D1474138

GOODBYE, CRUEL WORLD

Goodbye, Cruel World

An book of
memorable epitaphs

◆ **B O O K** ◆ **B L O C K S** ◆

This edition first published in 2004 by Book Blocks
an imprint of CRW Publishing Limited
69 Gloucester Crescent, London NW1 7EG

ISBN 1 904633 58 7

Text © CRW Publishing Limited 2004

1 3 5 7 9 10 8 6 4 2

Editorial selection by Rosemary Gray
Typeset in Great Britain by Antony Gray
Printed and bound in China by Imago

Contents

Chambers' caskets are just fine,
Made of sandalwood and pine –
If your loved ones have to go,
Call Columbus 690.
If your loved ones pass away,
Have them pass the Chambers way;
Chambers' customers all sing:
'Death, O death, where is thy sting?'

Dearest dust

My dearest dust, could not thy hasty day
Afford thy drowsy patience leave to stay
One hour longer: so that we might either
Sat up, or gone to bed together?
But since thy finished labour hath possest
Thy weary limbs with early rest,
Enjoy it sweetly: and thy widow bride
Shall soon repose here by thy slumbering side.
Whose business, now, is only to prepare
My nightly dress, and call to prayer:
Mine eyes wax heavy and the day grows old,
The dew falls thick, my beloved grows cold.
Draw, draw the closed curtains, and make room:
My dear, my dearest dust, I come, I come.

Epitaph to Sir William Dyer, d. 1641,
composed by his wife Catherine,
Colmworth, Bedfordshire

I coo and pine, and ne'er shall be at rest
Till I come to thee, dearest, sweetest and best.

St Michael's, Hartlip, Kent

Husband, I am waiting – April 1887
Wife, here I am – August 1925

from a cemetery in the South of France

O Death, all eloquent, you only prove
What dust we dote on when we creatures love.

from Eloisa to Abelard *by Alexander Pope*

This picture is for others, not for me,
For in my heart I wear thy memory;
It is here placed that passengers may know
Within thy grounds no weeds but corn did grow,
That there did flow within thy vital blood,
All that could make one honest, just and good;
Here is no elbow room to write of more,
An epitaph yields taste, but seldom more;
And now attend thee at the court in Heaven,
Thy work, sweet Charles, deserves the rarest wit –
Thy Jane for such a task is most unfit.

*at St Nicholas Aeons on the memorial of Charles
Rowyer, Alderman and Sheriff, 1580*

Youth, beauty, virtue heere inclos'd do lye,
Fate ne'er could boast so deare a victory.
'Twas heaven not death thus ravish'd her away,
For such perfection never could decay.
Her ashes in this monument must rest,
Her liveing tomb is in her husband's brest.

St James's, East Mailing, Kent

Dearest Thomas, thou art gone;
Thy kind heart I miss.
You did not say goodbye, Tom,
Or give me the parting kiss.

Rutland

Could grateful love recall the fleeting breath,
Or fond affection soothe relentless death,
Then had this stone ne'er claimed a social tear
Nor read to thoughtless man a lesson here.
As those we love decay, we die in part –
String after string, is sever'd from the heart.

1839

Go home, my wife, dry up your tears,
I am not dead, but sleeping here,
I am not yours, but Christ's alone –
He loved me best, to Him I've gone.

Fareham, Hampshire

A Husband kind, a Father dear,
A Friend in need lies buried here.

1855

She was . . .
But words are wanting to say what.
Think what a wife should be,
And she was that.

St Nicholas's, Southfleet, Kent

Lo! Where this silent marble weeps,
A friend, a wife, a mother sleeps.

1806

Where flies my wife, oh lovely once and fair,
Her face cast in the mould of beauty, where?
Her eyes all radiance, her cheeks like snow –
Those cheeks once tinctured with a purple glow?
Where those ivory teeth and lips of
celestial sound,
Her lips like lilys set with roses round?
Where's that soft marble breast, white neck,
and where
That all of woman past description fair?
All sunk, alas, in everlasting night.
Earth take her bones; chaste soul, she smiles
at rest
Whilst her image lives on immortal in my breast.

1779

Here lies Merrily Joules,
A beauty bright,
Who left Isaac Joules,
Her heart's delight.

Yatton, Somerset, 1827

O cruel death! how could you be so unkind
As to take him before and leave me behind?
Why didn't you take both of us, if either,
Which would have been better for the survivor?

Liverpool

My Ann, my all, my Angel Wife,
My dearest one, my love, my life,
I cannot sigh or say farewell –
But where thou dwellest I will dwell.

Williamsburg, Virginia, 1849

There's not an hour
Of day or dreaming night but I am with thee;
There's not a breeze but whispers of thy name,
And not a flower that sleeps beneath the moon
But in its fragrance tells a tale of thee.

for Jane Placide, American actress,
who died in 1835

Heer Leah's fruitfulness:
Heer Rachel's beauty:
Heer lyeth Rebecca's faith:
Heer Sarah's duty.

Lord Fairfax on his wife –
Otley, Yorkshire:

The Greatest Person
I Have Ever Known.

on Elizabeth Cothran,
who died in 1925, by her husband,
Francis E. Harrison

She never done a thing to
displease her Husband.

1859

She was more to me
Than I expected.

1882

Farewell, dear wife, my life is past;
My love to you while life did last,
And after me no sorrows take
But love my orphans for my sake.

1867

Here lies the man Richard
And Mary his wife,
Their surname was Pritchard,
They lived without strife;
And the reason was plain –
They abounded in riches,
They had no care or pain,
And the wife wore the breeches.

Bath Abbey

Here snug in grave my wife doth lie,
Now she's at rest and so am I.

Edinburgh

Here lie the remains of H. P. Nichol's wife,
Who mourned away her natural life;
She mourned herself to death for her man,
While he was in the service of Uncle Sam.

1863

Who far beneath this stone doth rest
Has joined the army of the blest.
The Lord has taken her to the sky
The Saints rejoice and so do I.
Tears cannot restore her; therefore I cry.

1892

Here lies my wife Polly, a terrible shrew,
If I said I was sorry, I should lie too.

Australia

This Post, as Finney's Legend saith,
Awoke a Scolding Wife from Death;
But when at length she ceas'd to breathe
And honest Finney ceas'd to grieve,
'Oh shun,' he said, as borne along
With solemn dirge and funeral song,
'Oh shun, my friends, that cruel Stump
that gave my dear so hard a Bump.'

On Finney's Post,
now to be seen in the Victoria and Albert
Museum. Finney was a Burton merchant whose
scolding wife fell into a trance and was taken as dead.
While she was being carried to the grave, the bier
struck against this door-post and she woke up. She
even lived for several years afterwards, to Finney's
regret, which he later recorded in these lines.

Here lies the body of Molly Dickie,
the wife of Hall Dickie, tailor.

Two Great Physicians first
my loving husband tried
to cure my pain,
in vain.
At last he got a third,
and then I died.

Cheltenham

We liv'd one and twenty years
As man and wife together:
I could no longer keep her here,
She's gone – I know not whither.
Could I but guess, I do protest
(I speak it not to flatter),
Of all the women in the world
I never would come at her.
Her body is bestowed well,
A handsome grave doth hide her;
And sure, her soul is not in hell –
The devil would ne'er abide her.
I rather think she's soar'd aloft,
For, in the last great thunder,
Methought I heard her very voice
Rending the clouds in sunder.

Essex marshes

Here lies Mary, the wife of John Ford,
We hope her soul is gone to the Lord;
But if for Hell she has changed this life,
She had better be there than be
                    John Ford's wife.

1790

A loving wife
And tender mother
Left this base world
To enjoy the other.

1801

At break of day
I took my clay
My wife her tay.
Now here we lay
For that one day
I took her tay
And she – my clay.

Stelling Parva, Kent

Here lies my Wife,
Here lies She.

Hallelujah!
Hallelujee!

Yorkshire

With graceful and engaging mien
She trod the carpet and the green,
With such refulgent virtues deckt
As gained her wide and warm respect.
Prim health sat blooming on her cheeks
Till Fortune play'd her cruel freaks;
Her limbs in tort'ring pains confin'd
That wreck'd her joints tho' not her Mind,
By faith and patience fortified
The rudest tempest to abide,
'Bove which she soar'd to realms of bliss
When Jesus hail'd her with a kiss.

1791

Fair, kind, and true! a treasure each alone:
A wife, a mistress, and a friend in one;
Rest in this tomb, raised at thy husband's cost,
Here sadly summing what he had and lost.
Come, virgins, ere in equal bands you join,
Come first, and offer at her sacred shrine;
Pray but for half the virtues of this wife,
Compound for all the rest with longer life;
And wish your vows, like hers, may
                                          be returned,
So loved when living, and when dead
                                          so mourned.

Dryden on Lady Frances Whitmore,
buried at St Mary's, Twickenham in 1690

She was a modest virgin and a wife,
Chaste to her husband in the married life.
A mirrour of her sex, a mother deare;
Mild to good children, to the bad severe.
A decent matron in her garb, her dress
Neither fantastique nor yet fashionless,
Her carriage sober; of a holy mind
And open hand, her speech to all was kind.
Her fame deserves in marble to remain,
Born of a generous stocke and born again.

Halford, Warwickshire

In blisse is hee,
Whom I lov'd best,
Thrice happy shee
With him to rest.

So shall I bee
With him I loved,
And he with mee
And both us blessed.

Love made me Poet,
And this I writt,
My heart did do yt
And not my wit.

Burford Church, Oxfordshire

My dear and beloved Wife,
Thou has left me to mourn thy sad loss,
And by the Blessing of God and Son,
I found another Wife.

Exeter

In Memory of Elizabeth,
who should have been
the Wife of Mr Simeon Palmer.

In Memory of Lidia,
ye wife of Mr Simeon Palmer.

twin stones, Rhode Island

Know all posterity
that in the year of grace 1792
the rambling remains of the above said
JOHN DALE
were laid upon his two wives.
This thing in life might cause some jealousy,
But here all three lie lovingly,
But from embraces here no pleasure flows,
Alike are here all human joys and woes.
Here old John's rambling Sarah no more fears
And Sarah's chiding John no longer hears.
A period's to all their toilsome lives:
The good man's quiet; still are both his wives.

Bakewell, Derbyshire

Near this place are interred the wives of
Richard Jessap: viz. Alice, who died on
Sept. 27th, 1716, aged 25; and Joanna,
who died on Aug. 31, 1720, aged 29.

How soon ye objects of my love
By death were snatcht from me;
Two loving matrons they did prove,
No better could there be.
One child the first left to my care,
The other left me three.
Joanna was beyond compare,
A Phoenix rare was she;
Heaven thought her sure too good to stay

A longer time on earth,
In childbed therefore as she lay,
To God resign'd her breath.

Rauceby Church, Lincolnshire

To the memory of my four wives,
who all died within the space of ten years,
but more pertickler to the last,
Mrs Sally Home, who has left me
and four dear children.
She was a goud, sober, and clean soule
and may i soon go to her.
A.D. 1732.
Dear wives, if you and i shall all
go to heaven, the Lord be blest,
for then we shall be even.
WILLIAM JOY HOME,
carpenter.

Kent

Here lies Hannah Church
and probably a portion of Emily.
Sacred to the memory of Emily Church,
who seems to be mixed with Matilda.
Stranger pause, and drop a tear,
for Emily Church lies buried here,
mixed in some perplexing manner
with Mary, Matilda, and
probably Hannah.

Composed by a New England man,
the remains of whose wives
had been moved and reinterred

Here lie my husbands – One, Two, Three –
Dumb as men ever could wish to be.
As for my Fourth, well, praise be God,
He bides for a little above the sod.
But his wit being weak and his eyeballs dim,
Heav'n speed at last I'll wear weeds for him.
Thomas, John, Henry, were these three's names,
And to make things tidy, I adds his – James.

Ireland

This turf has drank a widow's tear,
Three of her husbands slumber here.

Staffordshire

Bonds are all determinate

I want no crape to hang upon the door
                                 when I die;
I want no bell to tell the way to where I lie;
I want no sorrowful prayers upraised to
                                 Him on high;
I want no heart to sob nor any heart to cry.
I want the flowers, the bees, the birds to be
                          around the day I go;
I want a bird to sing his song of evening
                                soft and low;
I want a bee to buzz around the place I rest;
I want a flower to bloom upon the mound
                              atop my breast.

composed by the editor
of an American newspaper

Beneath this stone the best of parents lies,
In friendship constant, and in knowledge wise;
They died in humble hope, their trust in God –
Oh, may we follow in the steps they trod.

Hillingdon, Middlesex, 1864

Warm summer sun, shine kindly here;
Warm southern wind, blow softly here;
Green sod above, lie light, lie light –
Good-night, dear heart, good-night, good-night.

for Olivia Susan Clemens,
written by her father, Mark Twain, 1890

Father and Mother and I
Lies buried here asunder;
Father and Mother lies buried here
And I lies buried yonder.

Bude parish church

Mamma and I together lived
Just two years and a half.
Mamma went first, I followed,
The Cow before the Calf.

Dorset

God be praised!
Here lies Mr Dudley, senior,
And Jane, his wife, also,
Who, while living, was his superior;
But see what death can do!
Two of his sons also lie here,
One Walter, t'other Joe;
They all of them went, in the year 1510, below.

Broome churchyard, Worcestershire

Here lies the body of Thomas Vernon,
The only surviving son of Admiral Vernon.

Plymouth

At my right hand lies my son John,
As we did lay in bed,
And there do lay till Christ do say,
'Come ye out ye dead.'

Bishops Cannings churchyard, Wiltshire

Here lies the body of Joe Sewell,
Who to his wife was very cruel,
And likewise to his brother Tom,
As any man in Christendom.
And that's all I'll say of Joe –
Here he lies and let him go.

Great Cornard, near Sudbury, Suffolk

Who with all his faults
Loved his family and his fellow man.

Belstead, Suffolk

Here lies the body of Joan Cathew,
Born at St Columb, died at St Cue.
Children she had five,
Three are dead and two alive,
Those that are dead choosing rather
To die with their mother than live
                              with their father.

St Agnes, Cornwall

Here lies Jane Shore.
    I say no more.

1878

Sixty-three years our Hayman
Sailed merrily round;
Forty-four lived parishioner
Where he's Aground.
Five wives bore him thirty-three
Children enough;
Land another as honest
Before he Gets Off.

South Benfleet, Essex, dated 1728

Torn from the embraces of his second wife,
And their fond children, happy in his life,
Lost to the poor, too, who exclaim in woe,
Striking their bosoms, here lies Mr Yeo!

Bleadon, Somerset, 1763

Her lieth Ane: Forstr
Daughter and Heyr to
Thomas Gaynsford Esquier
deceased XVIII of Januari 1591
leavyng behind her
II sones and V daughters.

*This epitaph, upon its original stone, is used as a
fire-back in a public house at Billingshurst, Kent*

Here lies the body of a matriarch who had 13 children, 101 grandchildren, 274 great-grand-children, and 49 great-great-grandchildren. A total of 437 offspring. 336 survived her.

1768

In memory of Mrs Phoebe Crewe,
who died May 28, 1817, aged 77 years.
During 40 years as a midwife
in this City, she brought into
the world 9,730 children.

Norwich

Three Saffords out of view –
Mabel, Mary, Bartholomew –
Bartholomew Safford's flesh and bone,
His wife, his sister and his son.
Mabel became for worms a bait
December 9th in forty eight;
Mary was fitted for the bier
On March 4th that same year;
Death on Bartholomew did fixe
On March the 2nd forty six.
Husband, brother, father dear,
He is Christ's minister and pastor here.

Bicknoller, Somerset, 1662

The wine that in these earthen vessels lay,
The hand of death hath lately drawn away,
And as a present served it up on high,
Whilst heere the vessels with the Lees do lie.

from Branscombe in Devon on a father and son by the
name of Lee who were buried 'at one time together in
one grave' in 1658

John Palfreyman, which lieth here,
Was aged twenty-four year;
And near this place his mother lies,
Also his father when he dies.

Grantham, Lincolnshire

And how it made my bosom heave
To hear my sister cease to breathe,
When God, to carry out his plans,
Caused her to die within my hands.
And now, dear Saviour, please adore
Her mother, now aged eighty-four;
Look down upon her from on high
And bless her last breaths ere she die.

Eye, Suffolk

In memory of Polly,
mother of 200 pigs.
Died December 23rd., 1904, aged 15½ years.

Worsley, near Manchester

Below lyes for sartin'
Honest old Halting,
And snug close beside un
His fat Wife, a wide one;
If another you lack,
Look down and see Jack;
And farther a yard
Lyes Charles, who drank hard;
And near him is Sloggy,
Who never got groggy
Like Charles and his Father,
Too abstemious the rather,
And therefore popped off
In a tissicy cough.
Look round now and spy
The whole family lie.

Ditchling, Sussex

At once deprived of life, lies here
A family to vertue dear;
Tho' far removed from regal state,
Their virtues made them truly great.
Lest one should feel the others fall,
Death has in kindness seiz'd them all.

on a whole family cut off by smallpox

And in her memory we think we find
These accents uttered at this time.
Companions, you who once were mine,
Unto you I speak by the hand of time.
Yes! unto you who once were joined
Unto me by Friendship's coin,
Yea, unto you I now do speak,
Although my eyes are closed in sleep.
Here lies the remnants of your friend
Beneath this grassy mound;
And flowers may deck and flowers may bloom,
And flowers may wither on this mound,
Here stands my Tomb.

Washington, Connecticut

Here lie several of the Saunderses of this parish.
Further particulars the last day will disclose.
Amen.

Tetbury parish church

Here lies the body of Jonathan Tilton
Whose friends reduced him to a skeleton.
They robbed him out of all he had
And now rejoice that he is dead.

1837

Behold we see while here we look
The nearest ties of friendship broke;
The grief and sorrow pain the heart –
The dearest friends we see must part.

1849

Alas poor Beau,
Died February 28th, 1852.

It is but to a dog that this stone is inscribed.

Yet what now is left within
the home of thy fathers,
O solitary master, that will grieve for thy
departure, or rejoice at thy return?

E. B. L. [Edward Bulwer Lytton]

in the grounds of Knebworth Park, Hertfordshire

Here lies the great heart of a little dog
BUDGET,
who died 5 June 1886.

in the grounds of
Knebworth Park, Hertfordshire

IN MEMORY OF THE OLD FISH

Under the soil the old fish do lie,
Twenty years he lived and then did die.
He was so tame, you understand,
He would come and eat out of your hand.

Blockley, Worcestershire

ROSA

My first Jersey Cow,
who gave a record 2 lbs 15 ozs
of butter from 18 quarts of milk –
1 day's yield.

Evergreen Cemetery, Central Village, Connecticut

RASTAS
The smartest,
most lovable
Monkey
that ever lived.

Hartsdale, New York

Various the roads of life; in one
    All terminate, one lonely way.
We go; and, 'Is he gone?'
    Is all our best friends say.

Walter Savage Landor 1775–1864

Home, without a journey

Home – without a journey.

on the grave of a child at
Boughton Monchelsea, Kent

Into the world this little babe did peep,
Disliked it, closed its eyes and fell asleep.

from West Wycombe, Buckinghamshire,
on a child aged four months who died in 1830

When I came into this world
I found nothing worth my stay,
So I turned myself around
And went on my heavenly way.

to child a of three at Richmond

He tasted of life's bitter cup,
Refused to drink the potion up,
But turned his little head aside,
Disgusted with the taste, and died.

in a Devon churchyard

Happy the babe thus privileged by fate,
Given shorter labour and a lighter weight –
Received but yesterday the gift of breath,
Ordered tomorrow to return to death.

Yoxford, Suffolk

Came in,
Looked about;
Didn't like it,
Went out.

*on the headstone of a two-week-old baby
in a Suffolk village*

Early, bright, transient, chaste as morning dew,
They sparkled, were exhaled, and went
                                        to Heaven.

on a grave shared by two children at Whitby,
Yorkshire

Here lie the bodies of two infants dear,
One's buried at Connaught, the other here.

Highgate Cemetery

Here a pretty baby lies,
Sung asleep with lullabies;
Pray be silent and not stir
Th' easy earth that covers her.

Robert Herrick

The bud was spread
To show the rose;
Our Saviour smiled
The bud was closed.

Stamford, Lincolnshire

This lovely bud, so young and fair,
Call'd hence by early doom,
Just came to show how sweet a flower
In Paradise might bloom.

Richmond, Virginia

He plucked me like a tender flower,
From this world of faded light,
To dwell among the angels,
Up in heaven so fair and bright.

1859

To the memory of
JOHN MAGHI

An incomparable boy,
Who, thro' the unskilfulness of the midwife,
On the 21st day of December, 1532,
Was translated from the womb to the tomb.

Abney Park Cemetery, Stamford Hill

See here, nice Death, to please his palate,
Takes a young lettuce for a sallet.

epitaph on Laetitia, three years old

Our little Jacob has been taken from this earthly garden to bloom in a superior flower-pot above.

Maine, USA

Here lieth a blossom of the world's great tree, which was as fare as buds of roses. She died an infant. Heaven was made for such. Live like an infant, thou shalt have as much.

*from Branscombe, Devon,
in memory of Anna Bartlett,
who died in 1698*

My lovely little Tommy,
Thou wert gathered very soon –
In the fresh and dewy Morning
Not in the glare of Noon;
The Saviour sent his Angels
To bear thee hence, My Own,
And they'll plant thee in that Garden
Where decay is never known.

North Devon

Short was my time, the longer is my rest;
God took me hence because He thought it best.

1864

Beneath this stone our baby lies,
He neither cries nor hollers,
He lived just one-and-twenty-days,
And cost us forty dollars.

United States

How soon I was cut down,
When innocent at play!
The wind it blew a ladder down
And took my life away.

on a child's grave in Baldock, Hertfordshire

Harry Sisley of Kilburn, aged 10, drowned in attempting to save his brother, after he himself had been rescued, May 24, 1878.

Postman's Park, London EC1

Highly favoured probationer,
Accepted without being exercised.

from Southwold, Suffolk, on a baby

For yeares a childe, for
Sparkles of God's Grace
A Jewell Rich, Intombde
Lies in this Place;
Her Ashes (onelie) here; all ells
Is gone to Rest –
God takes them youngest, whom
He loveth best.

St Mary's, Mortlake, 1616

This innocence whose corpse lies here
It was Belov'd of Parents Dear.

1749

Jane Lister: Deare Child.

Westminster Abbey

This little darling that lies here
Was conquered by the diarrhoea.

1870

And death and envye both must say 'twas fitt
Her memory should thus in brasse bee writt.
Here lyes interr'd within this bed of dust
A virgin pure, not stained by carnall lust;
Such grace the King of Kings bestow'd upon her
That now shee lives with him, a maid of honour;
Her stage was short, her thread was quickly spunn,
Drawne out and cutt, for Heaven her worke was done.
This world to her was but a traged play,
She came and saw't, dislik't, and passed away.

on a child of ten, from St Saviour's,
Southwark, 1652

Farewell, thou child of my right hand, and joy.
Rest in soft peace and, ask'd, say here doth lie
Ben Jonson his best piece of poetry.

Ben Jonson, on his son

Sweet little darling, light of the home,
Looking for someone, beckoning come.
Bright as a sunbeam, pure as the dew,
Anxiously looking, Mother, for you.

Buckland Newton, Dorset

Long night succeeds thy little day
Oh! blighted blossom! can it be
That this grey stone and grassy clay
Have closed our anxious care of thee?
The half-formed words of liveliest thought
That spoke a mind beyond thy years;
The song, the dance by nature taught,

The sunny smiles, the transient tears;
The symmetry of face and form,
The eye with light and life replete;
The little heart so fondly warm,
The voice so musically sweet.
These lost to hope, in memory yet
Around the hearts that loved thee cling,
Shadowing with long and vain regret,
The too fair promise of thy spring.

composed by Thomas Love Peacock in
remembrance of his daughter Margaret,
who died in 1826 at the age of three
and was buried in Shepperton, Surrey

Hold, infidelity, turn pale and die,
Beneath this stone five infants' ashes lie;
Say, are they lost or saved?
If heaven's by works, in heaven they can't appear.
If death's by sin, they sinned because they are not here;
Reason – oh, how depraved!
Revere the sacred page, the knot's untied;
They died, for Adam sinn'd; they live, for Jesus died.

Brasted, Kent

Transplanted.

from a child's grave in
Hillmorton, Northamptonshire

No name have I, O Christ, to offer Thee,
Nor on my brow received the sacred sign,
Yet in the Book of Life remember me,
I plead my Saviour's name instead of mine.

on the grave of an unbaptised baby in Ingatestone
churchyard in Essex

Here lies the bodies of three children dear,
Two buried in the Isle of Wight and t'other here.
They was surprised by ague fits
And here they lays as dead as nits.

1899

Here lies Abraham, aged 17, and Charles, aged
13; the younger became involved in the tide,
when the elder plunged to his rescue. The
flood was stronger than their strength, though
not than their love, and as 'they were lovely
and pleasant in their lives', so 'in death they
were not divided'.

Clevedon, Somerset

The uplifted hand of death

But what security is breath
Against the uplifted hand of death?
Not one is safe, not one secure,
Not one can call his moments sure.

Yardley Old Church, Warwickshire

His last words were unspoken
He never said goodbye,
He was gone before he knew it
And only God knows why.

Cambridge

DONALD ROBERTSON

Born 11th January, 1785, died 4th June, 1848,
aged 63 years

He was a peaceable quiet man and to all appearances a sincere Christian. His death was very much regretted, which was caused by the stupidity of Laurence Tulloch in Clothester, who sold him nitre instead of Epsom salts, by which he was killed in the space of 3 hours after taking a dose of it.

Cross Kirk burial ground,
Esha Ness, Shetland

Here lie I and my three daughters
Killed by drinking Cheltenham waters,
Had we stuck to Epsom Salts
We'd not been lying in these 'ere vaults.

Cheltenham

Here lies the body of Mary Ann Lowder,
She burst while drinking a Seidlitz powder.
Called from this world to her heavenly rest,
She should have waited till it effervesced.

Burlington, Massachusetts, 1798

Alas Poor Willie! he is dead,
His friends know him no more,
For what he thought was H_2O
Proved H_2SO_4.

1982

She lived a life of virtue and died of cholera morbus, caused by eating green fruit, in the full hope of a blessed immortality at the early age of twenty-one years, seven months and sixteen days. Reader, go thou and do likewise.

East Tennessee

She was not smart, she was not fair,
But hearts with grief for her are swellin';
All empty stands her little chair –
She died of eatin' water melin.

New Jersey

Eliza, sorrowing, rears this marble slab
To her dear John, who died of eating crab.

Pennsylvania

Too wise, too good on earth to remain, so it pleased God (by the explosion of the powder mills) to take him back again.

1848

Sudden and unexpected was the end
Of our esteemed and beloved friend.
He gave to all his friends a sudden shock
By one day falling into Sunderland Dock.

Whitby churchyard

Here lies the body of James Hornbrick who was accidentally shot on the Pacer's River with one of the large Colt's revolvers with no stopper for the cock to rest on, it was one of the old-fashioned kind brass mounted and of such is the kingdom of Heaven.

San Diego

In memory ov
John Smith, who met
weirlent death neer this spot
18 hundred and 40 too. He was shot
by his own pistol.
It was not one of the new kind
but a old-fashioned
brass barrel, and of such is the
kingdom of heaven.

Sparta Diggins, California

Unto the mournful fate of young John Moore,
Who fell a victim to some villain's power
In Richmond Lane, near Aske Hall, 'tis said.
There was his life most cruelly betrayed,
Shot with a gun by some abandoned rake,
Then knocked o' th' head with a hedging stake.
His soul, I trust, is with the blest above,
There to enjoy eternal rest and love.
Then let us pray his murderer to discover,
That he to justice soon may be brought over.

Gilling, near Richmond, Yorkshire

Let this small monument record the name
Of Badman, and to future times proclaim
How, by an attempt to fly from this high spire
Across the Salrine stream, he did acquire
His fatal end. 'Twas not for want of skill,
Or courage to perform the task, he fell.
No, no! a faulty cord being drawn too tight
Hurried his soul on high to take her flight
And bid the body here good-night.
Feby 2nd, 1739. Aged 28.

epitaph on an early pioneer of flight,
St Mary's, Shrewsbury

Daniel Chappell
Who was killed in the act of taking a whale.

1845

In Memory of Hannah Trylyne
In bloom of life
She was snatched from hence,
She had not room
To make defence;
For tyger fierce
Snatched life away,
And here she lies in bed of clay
Until the Resurrection Day.

*in Malmesbury Abbey churchyard,
to a girl killed by a tiger that
escaped from a travelling show*

Sacred to the memory of
MAJOR JAMES BRUSH

who was killed by the accidental
discharge of a pistol by his orderly,
14th April, 1831.
Well done, thou good and faithful servant.

Woolwich churchyard

Here lies, cut down like unripe fruit,
The wife of the deacon Amos Shute;
She died of drinking too much coffee,
Anny Dominy Eighteen Forty.

Connecticut, 1840

In Memory of Samuel Barns,
Son of Mr Samuel Barns
and Mrs Welthy Barns,
whose Death was Occasion'd
by a Scald from a Tea pot.

New Haven, Connecticut, 1794

To all my friends I bid adieu,
A more sudden death you never knew.
As I was leading the old mare to drink,
She kick'd me and kill'd me quicker'n a wink.

New Hampshire, USA

The apple wheel did roll on me
And by it I was slain,
But Christ has bought my liberty,
In Him I'll rise again.

1799

On a Thursday she was born,
On a Thursday made a bride,
On a Thursday broke her leg,
And on a Thursday died.

Church Stretton in Shropshire, 1814

Here I lie and no wonder I'm dead,
I fell from a tree
And damaged my head.

1824

Here lies John Adams, who received a thump,
Right in the forehead from the parish pump.

Jersey

By spots he died tho' spotless was his life.

1767

Here lies John Ross
Kicked by a hoss.

Jersey

Sacred to the memory of Ebenezer Harvey, who died through being accidentally kicked by a cow on the l8th September 1853. Well done, thou good and faithful servant.

Boston

Here lies the body of Emily White,
She signalled left, and then turned right.

Here lie I, and no wonder I'm dead,
For the wheel of the waggon went over my head.

Pembrokeshire

Here lies an honest, independant man –
Boast more, ye great ones, if ye can.
I have been kicked by bull and ram;
Now let me lie contented as I am.

Ingham, Norfolk

IN MEMORIE OF THE CLERK'S SON

Bless my eyes,
Here I lies
In a sad pickle,
Killed by an icicle.

Bampton, Devon

The Lord saw good, I was lopping off wood
And down fell from the tree;
I met with a check, and I broke my neck
And so death lopped off me.

at Ockham, Surrey, dated 1736

Here lies the Body of Robert Moore –
What signifies more Words –
Who killed himself by eating of Curds;
But if he had been rul'd by Sarah his Wife
He might have lived all the Days of his Life.

from Dundalk churchyard in Ireland

Here lies John Higley, whose father and mother were drowned in their passage from America. Had they both lived they would have been buried here.

Belturbet, Ireland

Here lie the remains of Sarah Wills,
Who died of taking too many pills.
And just below
Lies Mr Crow,
Who died for love
Of the above.

Received of Philip Harding his borrowed earth, 1673.
O death,O death, thou hast cut down
The fairest Greenwood in the Town!
Her worth and amiable qualities are such
That she certainly deserved a Lord or Judge,
But her virtue and her great humility
Made her rather prefer a Doctor in Divinity.
For her and for all other good women's sake,
Never put a blister on a Lying-in Woman's back –
For in all such disorders anyone may chance to have,
It never fails to bring them to the Tomb or Grave.

Crudwell, Wiltshire

Nigh to the river Ouse, in York's fair city,
Unto this pretty maid Death showed no pitie;
As soon as she her pail of water fill'd,
Came sudden Death, and Life, like water, spill'd.

*St Mary's, York, on a woman accidentally drowned in
1696; the inscription was composed by her lover*

Here lies, free from blood and slaughter,
Once Underwood – now under water.

*in memory of Captain Underwood,
who was drowned*

Here lies one whose thread of life
was cut asunder –
She was stroke dead by a clap of thunder.

1719

Here lyeth ye body of
Sarah Bloomfield,
Aged 74.
Cut off in blooming yuthe,
We can but pity.

St Nicholas's, Yarmouth

Thomas Simpson died of exhaustion after saving many lives from breaking ice at Highgate ponds, January 25, 1885.

Postman's Park, London EC1

The body that here buried lies
By lightning fed death's sacrifice,
To him Elijah's fate was given –
He rode on flames of fire to heaven.
Then mourn no more he's taken hence
By the just hand of Providence –
O God, the judgments of Thy seat
Are wondrous good and wondrous great.
Thy ways in all Thy works appear
As thunder loud, as lightning clear.

from Tintagel in Cornwall, dated 1702

Between the remains of her brother Edward
And of her husband Arthur
Here lies the Body of Bridgett Applewhaite
Once Bridgett Nelson.
After the Fatigues of a Married Life
Borne by her with Incredible Patience
For four years and three Quarters, bating three weeks,
And after the Enjoiment of the Glorious Freedom
Of an easy and Umblemisht Widowhood
For four years and Upwards
She resolved to run the Risk of a Second Marriage Bed
But DEATH forbad the Banns –
And having with an Apoplectick Dart
(The same Instrument with which he had formerly

Dispacht her Mother)

Toucht the most vital part of her brain,

She must have fallen directly to the ground

(As one Thunder Strook)

If she had not been catcht and supported by her
intended Husband.

Of which invisible bruise

After struggle of above Sixty Hours

With that Grand Enemy to Life

(But the certain and Mercifull Friend to Helpless Old
Age)

In Terrible Convulsions, Plaintive Groans or
Stupefying Sleep,

Without recovery of her speech or Senses

She Dyed on the 12th day of Sept. of our Lord 1737
in Ye Year of her own age 44.

Behold I come as a Thief (Revelation, xiv:15),
But, O thou Source of Pious Cares,
Strict Judge without Regard,
Grant tho' we go hence unawares
We Go not Unprepared.
Amen.

Bramfield Parish Church, Suffolk

Here lie two brothers,
By misfortune surrounded,
One died of his wounds,
And the other was drownded.

Portsmouth, Hampshire

To the memory of Ric. Richards,
who by gang-green first lost a toe, afterwards a
leg, and lastly his life on 7th April, 1656.
Ah, cruel Death, to make three meals of one,
to taste and eat till all was gone!
But know, thou tyrant, when the trump shall call,
he'll find his feet, and stand when thou shalt fall.

Banbury churchyard, Oxfordshire

Molly, tho' pleasant in her day,
Was suddenly seized and went away.
How soon she's ripe, how soon she's rotten!
Laid in her grave, how soon forgotten!

1792

Think, my friends, when this you see,
How my wife has done for me.
She in some oysters did prepare
Some poison for my lot and fare,
Then of the same I did partake
And Nature yielded to its fate.
Before she my wife became,
Mary Felton was her name.

1860

Killed by an omnibus – why not?
  So quick a death a boon is.
Let not his friends lament his lot –
  *Mors omnibus communis.**

Henry Luttrell (1765–1851)

on a man run over by a bus

* *Death is common to all men.*

Here lies a man who was killed by lightning;
He died when his prospects seemed to be
    brightening.
He might have cut a flash in this world of
    trouble,
But the flash cut him, and he lies in the stubble.

on anonymous epitaph
on an anonymous victim

Here lies Elizabeth Wyse,
Killed by thunder sent from Heaven
in 16 hundred and seventy-seven.

Greyfriars, Edinburgh

Mr Gilman Spaulding
Was kill'd with an axe
By an insane Brother.

1842

The wedding day appointed was,
The wedding clothes provided,
But ere that day did come, alas!
He sickened, and he dieded.

Bideford, Devon

Through Poison strong he was cut off,
And brought to Death at last.
It was by his Apprentice Girl;
On whom there's sentence past.
Oh, may all People warning take,
For she was Burned to a stake.

Portlemouth Church, South Devon

Here lie the bones of a poor dog,
Renowned for faith and bravery;
He died by hostile hands incog.,
His name was Pompey Savery.

Massachusetts

Died of thin shoes.

New Jersey, dated 1839

These walls, adorned with monumental busts,
Show how Bath waters serve to lay the dust.

Bath Abbey

Here lies one who came to this city
and died for the benefit of his health.

near Cincinnati

Stop, reader, pray and read my fate,
What caused my life to terminate,
For thieves by night when in my bed
Broke in my house and shot me dead.

Fawley churchyard, Hampshire

His illness laid not in one spot
But through his frame it spread,
The fatal disease was in his heart
And water in his head.

Whitby, Yorkshire, 1852

Under this stone lies the remain,
Who in Bromsgrove was slain.
A currier with his knife did the deed,
And left me in the street to bleed.
But when the Archangel's trump shall sound,
And souls to bodies join, that murderer
I trust shall see my soul in heaven secure.

Bromsgrove, Worcestershire

Here lies William Smith –
And what is something rarish,
He was born, bred, and hanged in this parish.

1798

GEORGE JOHNSON
Hanged by Mistake

As nurses strive their babes in bed to hie,
When they too liberally the wantons play;
So, to prevent his future grievous crimes,
Nature, his nurse, got him to bed betimes.

Bramley, Kent

Our life hangs on a single thread,
Which soon is cut & we are dead.
Then boast not, reader, of thy might –
Alive at noon & dead by night.

Thomas Warner,
died 4 September 1787,
aged fifty-three

Gone to do nothing for
ever and ever

Here lies an old woman who always was tired –
She lived in a house where help was not hired.
Her last words on earth were, 'Dear friends,
     I am going
Where washing ain't done, nor cooking, nor
     sewing.
Everything there will be just to my wishes –
For where they don't eat there's no washing of
     dishes.
I know that loud anthems will always be ringing,
But having no voice I'll be clear of the singing.
Don't fret for me now, don't fret for me never,
I'm going to do nothing for ever and ever.'

epitaph to one released from household drudgery

Here lies a great sleeper, as everybody knows,
Whose soul would not care if his body ne'er rose.
The business of life he hated, and chose
To die for his ease for his better repose;
And 'tis believed, when the last trump doth
                                    wake him,
Had the Devil a bed, he would pray him
                                    to take him.

epitaph on a great sleeper
by Sir Aston Cokayne 1608–84

Here Woollett rests, expecting to be saved;
He grav'd well, but now is well engraved.

on an engraver buried at St Pancras in 1785

A Master Printer of the Press, he spake
By mouth of many thousand tongues; he swayed
The pens which break the sceptres. Good Lord,
   make
Thy strong ones faithful and Thy bold afraid.

Sir Edwin Arnold on Edward Lloyd, 1890,
in St Margaret's, Westminster

Here lie the Mortal Remains of John Hulm,
    Printer,
Who, like an old worn-out Type, battered by
    frequent use,
Reposes in the grave
But not without a hope that at some future time
He might be
Recast in the Mould of Righteousness
And safely locked up
In the blissful Chase of Immortality.
He was distributed from the Board of Life,
On the 9th day of Sep. 1827,
Aged 75 years.

St Michael's, Coventry

Here lie the remains of L. Gedge, Printer.
Like a worn-out character,
He has returned to the Founder,
Hoping that he will be recast in a better
And more perfect mould.

Bury St Edmunds

Here Lyeth Thomas Peirce, whom no man
    taught
Yet he in Iron, Brasse, and silver wrought;
He Jacks, and Clocks, and watches (with Art)
    made,
And mended too when other worke did fade.
Of Berkeley five tymes Mayor this artist was,
And yet this Mayor, this Artist, was but grasse.
When his own Watch was Downe on his last
    Day,
He that had made watches had not made a key
To wind it Up, so Uselesse it must lie,
Until he Rise Againe no more to die.
Deceased 26 Aprill 1655, aetatis 77.

Berkeley, Gloucestershire

Here lies one who strove to equal time!
A task too hard, each power too sublime,
Time stopt his motion, o'erthrew his balance
     wheel,
Wore off his pivots, though made of hardened
     steel,
Broke all his spring, the verge of life decay'd,
And now he is as though he'd ne'er been made.
Not for the want of oiling that he tried,
If that had done, why then he ne'er had died.

parish church of St James's, Great Grimsby

Bilbie, thy
Movements kept in play
For thirty years or more,
They say.
Thy Balance or thy
Mainspring's broken,
And all thy movements
Cease to work.

Oxbridge, dated 1767

Here lies in a horizontal position the outside case of Thomas Hind, clock and watchmaker, who departed this life wound up in hope of being taken in hand by his Maker. Thoroughly cleaned, repaired, and set agoing for the world to come.

Bolsover, Derbyshire

Here lies a finished artist

on a painter

Here lies in horizontal position the outside case
    of George Routleigh, watchmaker,
Whose abilities in that line were an honour to
    his profession;
Integrity was the mainspring and prudence the
    regulator
Of all the actions of his life. Humane, generous
    and liberal,
His hand never stopped till he relieved distress.
Sincerely regulated were all his movements,
That never went wrong except when set agoing
By people who did not know his key;
Even then he was easily set right again.
He had the art of disposing his time so well
That his hours glided away in one continual
round of pleasure and delight –

Till an unlucky moment put a period to his
   existence.
He departed this life November 14th, 1802,
   aged 57
Wound up in hopes of being taken in hand
   by his Maker,
And of being thoroughly cleansed, repaired
And set agoing in the world to come.

Lydford, Devon

A zealous Locksmith died of late,
And did arrive at heaven's gate;
He stood without and would not knock,
Because he meant to pick the lock.

Mildred churchyard

Underneath this stone doth lye
The bodye of Mr Humpherie
Jones, who was of late
By trade a plate
Worker in Barbicanne;
Well known to be a good manne
By all his friends and neighbours too,
Who paid every bodie their due,
He died in the year 1737,
August 10th, aged 80; his soule, we hope's
In heaven.

from St Pancras churchyard

My Trip is Ended.
Send My Samples Home.

final instructions of a salesman who died in 1862

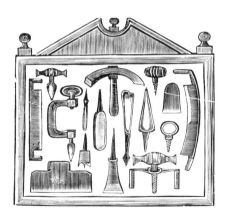

Beneath this stone lies Kathleen Grey,
Changed to a lifeless lump of clay;
By earth and clay she got her pelf,
And now she's turned to earth herself.
Ye weeping friends, let me advise,
Abate your tears and dry your eyes;
To what avails a flood of tears?
Who knows but in a course of years
In some tall pitcher or brown pan
She in her shop may be again.

on the owner of a crockery shop in Chester

She was an indulgent mother, and the best of
   wives;
She brought into this world more than three
   thousand lives.

on Margaret Hawtree, a midwife, who died in 1734

Here lies one, believe it if you can,
Who, though an attorney, was an honest man.

St Mary's-le-Wyford. Lincolnshire

Robert Lives Esquire a Barrister so great a
lover of peace that when a contention arose
between Life and Death he immediately
yielded up the Ghost to end the dispute.

Richmond, Surrey

Here lies Robert Trollop
Who made yon stones roll up;
When death took his soul up
His body filled this hole up.

in Gateshead churchyard, on an architect

Youth Builds for Age,
Age Builds for Rest;
They who Build for Heaven
Build Best.

Peterborough Cathedral

Stranger, approach this spot with gravity,
John Brown is filling his last cavity.

on the grave of a dentist

Here lie the remains of John Hall, grocer. The world is not worth a fig and I have good raisins for saying so.

Dunmore, Ireland

Like to a baker's *oven* is the grave
Wherein the bodyes of the faithful have
A *setting in*, and where they do remain
In hopes to *rise*, and to be *drawn* again;
Blessed are they, who in the Lord are dead,
Though set like *dough*, they shall be drawn
                like *bread*.

Christ Church, Bristol

Underneath this crust,
Lies the mouldering dust
Of Eleanor Batchelor Shoven,
Well versed in the arts
Of pies, custards, and tarts,
And the lucrative trade at the oven.
When she'd lived long enough,
She made her last puff,
A puff by her husband much praised;
And now she doth lie,
And make a dirt pie,
In hopes that her crust may be raised.

on a Yorkshire cook

WILLIAM SYMONS
ob. 1753, aet. 80

Here lies my corpse, who was the man
That loved a sop in a dripping pan.
But now, believe me, I am dead,
See here the pan stands at my head.
Still for sops to the last I cried,
But could not eat and so I died.
My neighbours, they perhaps will laugh
When they do read my epitaph.

Wood Ditton, Cambridgeshire.
The pan referred to was fixed to the
gravestone in accordance with
the writer's instructions.

Here lieth Tho. Turar and Mary, his wife. He was twice Master of the Company of Bakers, and twice Churchwarden of this parish. He died March 6th, 1654. She died May 8th, 1643.

In Memory of
JOHN BUCKETT,
many years landlord of the
Kings Head Inn in this Borough, who
departed this life November 25th, 1802,
Aged 67 years. And is alas! poor
BUCKETT
gone? Farewell, convivial Honest
JOHN!
Oft at the well by Fatal stroke
Buckets like pitchers must be broke –
In this same motley shifting scene
How various have thy fortunes been!
Now lifted high, now sinking low,
Today thy brim would overflow;
Thy bounty then would all supply

To fill & drink & leave thee dry.
Tomorrow sunk as in a well,
Content unseen with Truth to dwell,
But high, or low, or wet or dry,
No rotten stave could malice spy.
Then rise, immortal Buckett, rise
And claim thy station in the skies –
'Twixt Amphora & Pisces shine,
Still guarding Stockbridge with thy sign.

Stockbridge churchyard, Hampshire

Here repose Victor and Annette Poulard, faithful spouses and good tavern keepers. May the Lord welcome them as they received their guests.

at Mont St Michel, Brittany,
to restaurateurs famed for their omelettes

Beneath this stone, in hopes of Zion,
Doth lie the landlord of the Lion.
His son keeps on the business still,
Resigned unto the heavenly will.

Upton-on-Severn, Gloucestershire

G. Winch, the brewer, lies buried here;
In life he was both 'ale and stout.
Death brought him to his bitter bier;
Now in Heaven he hops about.

epitaph for a brewer

Joseph Thackrey by name,
Who, by the help of God,
Brought Sulphur Wells to fame.
In the year of our Lord 1740
I came to the Crown;
In 1791 they laid me down.
When I shall rise again
No man can surely tell;
But in hope of heaven,
I'm not afraid of hell.
To friends I bid farewell
And part without a frown,
In hopes to rise again
And have a better Crown.

parting words of an erstwhile landlord of
the Crown Inn, Pannal, Yorkshire

Here lies John Higgs,
A famous man for killing pigs,
For killing pigs was his delight
Both morning, afternoon, and night.
Both heats and cold he did endure,
Which no physician could ere cure.
His knife is laid, his work is done;
I hope to Heaven his soul has gone.

Cheltenham

My sledge and hammer be reclined,
My bellows too have lost their wind;
My fire's extinguished, forge decay'd,
And in the dust my vice is laid.
My iron's spent, my coals are gone,
The last nail's drove, my work is done.

blacksmith of Chesthunt, Hertfordshire,
who died in 1826

Here lyeth John Cruker, a maker of bellowes;
He was craftes-master and king of good fellowes.
Yet when he came to the hour of his death
He that made bellowes could not make breath.

from an Oxford churchyard

Here lies John Hyde –
First he lived and then he died.
He dyed to live and lived to die,
And hopes to live eternally.

1804

The engine now is cold and still,
No water does my boiler fill;
My coke affords its flame no more,
My days of usefulness are o'er;
My wheels deny their noted speed,
No more my guiding hand they heed,
My whistle too has lost its tone,
Its shrill and thrilling sounds are gone.
My valves are now thrown open wide,
My flanges all refuse to guide
My clacks, which now though once so strong
Refuse to aid the busy throng.
No more I feel each urging breath,
My steam is now condensed in death.
Life's railway o'er each station's past,
In death I'm stopped and rest at last.

Forget, dear friends, and cease to weep –
In Christ I'm safe, in Him I sleep.

*under the design of a locomotive in Newton-le-
Willows parish churchyard, Lancashire*

No more will he stand on the foot-plate,
No more will he steam into town,
He has shut off his steam for ever,
And gone to pick up his crown.

*commemorating a man
thought to have been a driver on an
armoured train during the siege of Kimberley*

Whyllst I lyved, I lyved to dye,
Now I live in Church eternilly.
Some I spent, much I gave,
What I lent, now I have.

Thurleston, Devon

Here lies a man who first did dye
When he was twenty-four,
And yet he lived to reach the age
Of hoary hairs fourscore;
And now he's gone, and certain 'tis
He'll not die any more.

St Nicholas's, Great Yarmouth

Cotton and calicos, all adieu,
And muslins, too, farewell,
Plain, striped, and figured old and new,
Three quarter, yard or ell;
By nail and yard I've measured ye
As customers inclined,
The churchyard now has measured me
And nails my coffin bind.

epitaph for a draper

In memory of
JONATHAN SOUTHWARD
BUTCHER
who died Feby 19th, 1727, aged 37.

By this Inscription be it understood
My occupation was in shedding blood;
And many a beast by me was weekly slain,
Hunger to ease and Mortals to maintain.
Now here I rest from sin and sorrow free
By means of Him who shed His blood for me.

Colerne Church, Wiltshire

John Adams lies here, of the parish of Southwell,
A carrier who carried his can to his mouth well;
He carried so much and he carried so fast
He could carry no more, so was carried at last:
For the liquor he drunk being too much for one,
He could not carry off, so is now carrion.

Nottinghamshire, 1852

Here lies Will Salter, honest man –
Deny it, envy, if you can.
True to his business and his trust,
Always punctual, always just;
His horses, could they speak, would tell
They loved their good old master well.
His uphill work is chiefly done,
His stage is ended, race is run;
One journey is remaining still,
To climb up Zion's holy hill.

at Haddiscoe, near Lowestoft

My Horses have done running,
My Waggon is decayed,
My body in the dust is laid.
My whip is worn out,
And my work it is done,
And I am brought here to my last home.

Palgrave churchyard, Suffolk

I in my time did gather rags
And in my time did fill my bags;
Although it was a ragged trade,
My rags are sold, my debts are paid:
Therefore go on, don't waste your time
On bad biography and bitter ryme;
What I am this cumbrous clay assures,
And what I was is no affair of yours.

to one Samuel Pears, who died in 1809 in
Wymondham, Leicestershire

Here lie the bones of William Jones,
Who when alive collected bones,
But Death – that bony grizzley spectre,
That most amazing bone collector –
Has boned poor Jones so snug and tidy,
That here he lies in bona fide.

Hurrah, my boys, at the parson's fall,
For if he'd lived he'd a buried us all.

South Wales

He that carried many a body brave
Was carried by a fever to the grave.
He carried – and was carried – that's even!
Lord, make him Porter to the gates of Heaven.

Clun, Shropshire

Here lies within this Porch so calm
Old Thomas, pray sound his knell,
Who thought no song was like a Psalm,
No music like a Bell.

in Rothwell churchyard, Yorkshire,
on a dedicated sexton

The vocal powers here let us mark,
Of Philip, our late Parish clerk.
In church none ever heard a layman
With a clearer voice say Amen.
Who now with Hallelujah's sound
Like him can make the roof rebound?
The choirs lament his choral tones,
The town so soon – here lie his bones.

Bakewell, Derbyshire

Here lies the Earl of Suffolk's fool,
Men call'd him Dicky Pearce;
His folly serv'd to make folks laugh,
When wit and mirth were scarce.
Poor Dick alas is dead and gone,
What signifies to cry?
Dickys enough are still behind,
To laugh at by and by.

Berkeley, Gloucestershire

Stephen and time are now both even:
Once Stephen beat time
Now time beats Stephen.

on a village choirmaster

The Life of this Clerk was just threescore and ten,
Nearly half of which time he had sung out Amen.
In his youth he was married like other young men,
But his Wife died one day so he chaunted Amen.
A second he took, she departed – what then?
He married and buried a third with Amen.
Thus his joys and his sorrows were Treble, but then
His voice was deep Bass as he sang out Amen.
On the Horn he could blow as well as most men,
So his Horn was exalted in blowing Amen.
But he lost all his Wind after threescore and ten,
And here with three Wives he waits till again
The Trumpet shall rouse him to sing out Amen.

on a tombstone raised by the inhabitants of Crayford
to the clerk of the parish who died on his way to assist
at a wedding in 1811

Snug neath this wall lies old Sam Cook,
Who with his spade his bell and book
Served sexton three score years and three,
Until his master grim death cried:
Enough, thy book now lay aside
And let a Brother bury thee.

Blyth, Northumberland

This man he got his livelihood
By hewing faggots and felling wood.
Till Death, the conqueror of all,
Gave the feller himself a fall.

Brinklow, Warwickshire

Under this stone lies Meredith Morgan,
Who blew the bellows of our church organ;
Tobacco he hated, to smoke most unwilling,
Yet never so pleased as when pipes he was filling.
No puffer was he,
Though a capital blower,
He could fill double G
And now he's a note lower.

Ruthin, North Wales

Sacred to the Memory of

THOMAS HALL

Late Organist of Holy Trinity in this town,
who died June 19th, 1837, aged 36 years.

Just like an Organ robb'd of Pipes and Breath,
Its Keys and Stops all useless made by Death,
In dust and quite motionless its ruins laid,
Although 'twas built by more than mortal aid;
But when new tuned, this instrument shall raise
To God, its builder, endless songs of praise.

Warrington parish churchyard

Beneath this stone Old Michael lies at rest;
His rustic rig, his song, his jug, were ever of the best.
With nodding head the choir he led
That none might start too soon,
His viol too he played full true,
His voice it kept the tune.
And when at length his age had passed
Three score years less eleven,
With faithful cling to fiddle's string
He sang himself to heaven.

from a Sussex churchyard

Here lies
JANE SMITH,
wife of Thomas Smith, marble cutter.

This monument was erected by her husband as a tribute to her memory and a specimen of his work. Monuments of the same style, 350 dollars.

near Cincinnati

Near to this stone lies Archer (John),
Late Saxon (I aver),
Who, without tears, thirty-four years
Did carcases inter.
But Death at last for his works past
Unto him then did say,
Leave off thy trade, be not afraid
But forthwith come away.
Without reply or asking why,
The summons he obeyed,
And in seventeen hundred and sixty-eight.
Resigned his life and spade.

Selby Abbey

Father Time has knocked him down, but
he will rise again in the resurrection.

to Sir Richard Parkins,
a famous wrestler of his day

Death took him in the Upper View
And gave him such a Brace,
The grapple turned him black and blue
And made him shift his place.
Parts of Access he next assailed
With such a Knock-down blow
As never yet to mortals fail'd
A total overthrow.

on a well-known wrestler and boxer

Here lies James Earl, the Pugilist,
Who, on the 11th of Aprill, 1788,
Gave in.

Oundle, Northamptonshire

He bowled his best but was himself
bowled by the best on July 2nd, 1912.

Tom Richardson, England cricketer,
who died in 1912

Here lie the poor bones of Bryan Tunstall.
He was a most expert angler
Until Death, envious of his merits,
Threw out his line, hook'd him and
Landed him here, 21st April 1790.

Ripon, Yorkshire

In wise frugality luxuriant,
In justice and good acts extravagant;
To all ye world a universal friend,
No foe to any but of ye savage kind;
How many fair estates have been erased
By ye same gen'rous means, yet his increased,
His duty thus performed to heaven and earth;
Each leisure hour great toilsome sports gave birth,
Had Nimrod seen, he would ye game decline,
To Gilbert mighty hunter's name resign;
Though hundreds to ye ground he oft has chac'd,
That subtile fox, death, earth'd him here at last,
And left a fragrant scent so sweet behind,
That ought to be persu'd by all mankind.

in Cantley Church, Norfolk,
a tribute to a fox-hunting squire who died in 1714

Here lies a huntsman, who was stout and bold,
His judgement such as could not be controll'd.
Few of his calling could with him compare,
For skill in hunting fox or fallow deer.
He shewed his art in England, Ireland and France,
And rests in this churchyard, being his last chance.

to the memory of one Ned Baldrey

To the memory of Mr Carter, to whom the
poor of this town have been indebted for
170 years for the gifts of cloaks and coats,
annually distributed on St Thomas's Day.
Traveller – I will relate a wonderous thing.
On the day upon which the above-mentioned
THOS CARTER
breathed out his soul, a Sudbury camel
went through the eye of a needle!
Go, and should you be rich,
do likewise. Farewell.

Sudbury, Suffolk

He is gone to that Place where only his
fireworks can be exceeded.

Inscription on the tomb of a
pyrotechnichal expert composed,
at the request of his widow, after Purcell's
epitaph in Westminster Abbey, which avers that
the musician had 'gone to that Blessed Place
where only his Harmony can be exceeded'.

He lies the corpse of Doctor Chard,
Who fill'd half of this churchyard.

Cornwall

A glassblower lies here at rest
Who one day burst his noble chest
While trying, in a fit of malice,
To blow a second Crystal Palace.

epitaph composed by J. B. Morton, b. 1893

A vein of gold

Here lies a piece of Christ, a star in dust,
A vein of gold, a china dish which must
Be us'd in Heav'n, when God shall feed the just.

St Martin's, Herne, Kent

To live in the hearts of those
we leave behind is not to die.

Lytham St Anne's, Lancashire

Sacred to the memory of
MRS MARY SANDERSON,
late of the Queen's House, London, who departed
this life 8th February 1783, aged 38. This stone
was erected by her disconsolate friends as a token
of the respect they owed to so amiable a woman:

In love she lived, in friendship died;
Her life was asked, but God denied.
We boast no virtues, nor beg any tears,
Yet, reader, if thou hast but eyes and ears,
It is enough. Oh! tell me why
Thou cam'st to gaze. Is it to pry
Into our loss? or borrow
A copy of our sorrow?
Or dost thou come to learn to die,
Knowing not whom to profit by?

If this be thy desire,
Then draw thee one step nigher.
Here lies a precedent, a fairer
Earth never showed, nor Heaven a rarer.
She was – but room forbids to tell thee what.
Sum all perfections up, and she was that.

Acton, Suffolk

Here lies John Auricular,
Who in the ways of the
Lord walked perpendicular.

New England

Plain, neat, just, liberal, chatty, droll,
At once a classic and convivial soul.
By native temper formed to suit the end
Of Husband, Parent, Neighbour, and of Friend.
Alike removed from meanness and from pride,
He lived respected and lamented died.

on Matthew Thomas, Hereford, 1796

Near this a rare jewell's set,
Closed up in a Cabinet,
Let no sacrilegious hand
Breake through – 'tis stricte command
Of the jeweller, who hath say'd
(And 'tis fit to be obeyed)
I'll require it safe and sound
Both above and under ground.

Fowey, Cornwall

Underneath this stone doth lie
As much beauty as could die.

from Ben Jonson's 'Epitaph for Lady H'

Deposited beneath are the remains of
SARAH BIFFIN,
who was born without Hands or Arms at East
Quantoxhead, County of Somerset, 25th Oct.,
1784; died at Liverpool, 2nd Oct., 1850.

Few have passed through the Vale of Life
so much the child of hapless fortune as
the deceased and yet possessed of mental
endowments of no ordinary kind.

Gifted with singular talents as an Artist,
thousands have been gratified with the
able productions of her pencil, while her
versatile conversation and agreeable
manners elicited the admiration of all.

This tribute to the memory of one so
universally known is paid by those who

were best acquainted with the character it so briefly portrays.

To any enquirers otherwise the answer is supplied in the solemn admonition of the Apostle, in 1 Corinthians, IV:5.

St James's Cemetery, Liverpool

Alice Ayres, daughter of a bricklayer's labourer, who by intrepid conduct saved three children from a burning house in Union Street, Borough, at the cost of her own young life.

Postman's Park, London EG24CI

Here, in peaceful silence, rest the remains of a man who never rose from his pillow in enmity to any human being; who he was it is needless to name, for if the kind recollections of his friends embalm not his memory, a tomb to record his name were vain indeed.

epitaph written shortly
before his death by Exuperious Pickering,
Llantysilio churchyard, Denbighshire

Sacred to the Memory of
MRS MARIA BOYLE,
who was a good Wife, a devoted Mother
and a kind and charitable Neighbour. She
painted in Water Colours and was First
Cousin to the Earl of Cork, and of such is
the Kingdom of Heaven.

Bandon, Ireland

G. L. NORRIS
never knew his advice to go wrong.

Here lie the remains of G. L. Norris, who
lived and died the happiest man on earth,
who was always busy doing good and trying
to do good, and advising and helping
those in trouble.

on a Penarth merchant who died in 1924

The sweet remembrance of the just
Shall flourish when they sleep in dust.

1776

She was Sober, Dilligent,
Honest and Vertuous,
And never was caught in a Lye,
Rare character in these degenerate days.

on a servant who died in 1774
and was buried at Acton

Here lies that happy maiden, who often said
That no man is happy until he is dead;
That the business of life is but playing the fool,
Which hath no relation to saving the soul:
For all the transaction that's under the sun,
Is doing of nothing, if that be not done –
All wisdom and knowledge does lie in this one.

*Barnes churchyard, on Anne Baynard, who died in
1696 at the age of 25. She was an earnest student of
theology and learned Greek in order to read St
Chrysostom in the original.*

Here lyes one worthie man
JOHN CONQUEROUR
who died Bailie of Pearth
the first day of Septm. 1653.

Ore death a conquerour here lyes, whose soule,
Freed from this dust, triumphs above the pole.
One less than twyce twelve children by ane wife
Hee had, of which to everlasting lyfe
Twice ten hee sent before him, and behynd
Hee left but three to propogate his kynd.
Hee ran ten lusters out when rigid fate
Robbed him of lyfe, pearth of a magistrate.

Greyfriars' graveyard, Perth

The lodging of all heavenly virtue is
Lodged here on earth whose soul has traviled
To Heaven in childbirth, and being brought to
     the bed
Of rest eternal she hath left behind her this
Her precious body which interred is.
The 4th day after Baptism had begun
The Resurrection of her newborn son.
She now hath found it true that childbirth pains
By faith, through death, life and salvation gains.

Barkway Church, Hertfordshire

Richly embalm'd indeed thou art,
In the mausoleum of the heart.

Nantucket, Massachusetts, 1851

Beneath this stone there lieth one
Who all his friends did please;
To Heaven we hope he's surely gone,
To enjoy eternal ease.
He drank, he sang, while here on earth,
Lived happy as a lord,
And now he hath resigned his breath,
God rest him, Paddy Ward.

Clogher Head, County Louth, Ireland

Here lies a careful, saving wife,
A tender, nursing mother;
A neighbour free from brawl and strife,
A pattern for all other.

Warrington parish churchyard, Lancashire

Here lies the body of Mary Gwynne,
Who was so very pure within;
She cracked the shell of her earthly skin
And hatched herself a Cherubim.

Cambridge

Lament, Reader, the Loss of a Pleasure
which his Contempt of human Applause
denies thee by commanding that this Marble
should not express his Amiable Character.

Barkway Church, Hertfordshire

This maid no elegance of form possessed,
No earthly love defiled her maiden breast,
Hence, free she lived from the deceiver, Man,
Heaven meant it for a blessing she was plain.

Warrington parish churchyard,
Lancashire, 1816

Underneath this sable hearse
Lies the subject of all verse:
Sidney's sister, Pembroke's mother,
Death, ere thou hast slain another
Wise and good and fair as she,
Time will throw his dart at thee.

Ben Jonson, on the Countess Dowager
of Pembroke, who died in 1621

Sacred to the memory of the inestimable
worth, unrivalled excellence and virtue of
N. R., whose ethereal parts became seraphic,
May 25th, 1767.

Litchfield, Connecticut

MARY BROOMFIELD,

dy'd 19th Novr 1788, aged 80 years

The chief concern of her life for the latter years was to order and provide for her funeral. Her greatest pleasure was to think and talk of it. She lived many years on a Pension of 9*d.* a week and yet saved £5, which at her own request was laid out in her burial. Reader, think not this short history useless. Excuse what thou mayest think folly, and, by her example, learn a lesson of the greatest wisdom to be mindful of thy latter end.

Macclesfield parish church

Taunton bore him, London bred him,
Piety trained him, vertue led him.
Earth enrich'd him, Heaven caress'd him.
This thankful town, that mindful city,
Share his piety and his pity.
What he gave, and how he gave it,
Ask the poor and you shall have it.
Gentle reader, Heaven may strike
Thy tender heart to do the like.
And now your eyes have read this story,
Give him the praise and Heaven the glory.

Robert Gray,
buried in Taunton, Somerset

This humble stone, what few vain marbles can,
May safely say – here lies an honest man.

Unitarian churchyard, Swansea

Here honest Sarah Ricketts lies,
By many much esteem'd,
Who really was no otherwise
Than what she ever seemed.

Barking, Essex, 1767

Here lies the carcase
Of honest John Parkhurst,
Who ne'er could dance or sing,
But was a faithful servant to his
Sovereign lord and king,
Charles the First.

Epsom parish churchyard

Her manners mild, her temper such!
Her language good, and not too much.

Wesleyan Chapel, Wakefield

The dame that rests within this tomb
Had Rachel's beauty, Leah's fruitful womb,
Abigail's wisdom, Lydia's faithful heart,
Martha's just care and Mary's better part.

1750

Beneathe this stone John Sayre the younger sleeps
Whilst saints on hie his soule in safety keepes;
In judgement, old; in yeares, in nature's prime;
Thus, reader, see, bothe younge and old he died.
Could wisdome, lore, or learninge purchase breath,
Thou hadst not died, nor wee bewayl thy deathe;
But, reader, marke the reason thou shalt finde,
Heaven takes the best, still leaves the worste behind.

St Mary's, Woodbridge, Suffolk

God takes the good, too good on earth to stay;
He leaves the bad, too bad to take away.

Gravesend, Kent

He that's here interred needs no versifying –
A virtuous life will keep the name from dying;
He'll live, though poets cease their
                              scribbling rhyme,
When that this stone shall moulder'd be by time.

1709

Alas, sweet Blossom, short was the period
that thy enlivening virtues contributed to
the Happiness of all thy connections, but
oh! how long have they to mourn the loss of
so much worth and Excellence.

Plymouth, Massachusetts, 1830

Wisht ashes were it piety to pray
Thy soule might once again informe thy clay;
Each holy tongue a prayer booke would penn
And force the heavens to send thee backe agen.
I blame thy goodness since 'tis understoode
Thou dyedst so soon because thou wert so good.
Say heavens when ye did want a saints supply
Did we not send a royal subsidy –
This Moyle more treasure to their glory brings
Than the proud camells of the Arabian kings.

All Saints, Boughton Aluph, Kent

Here a solemn fast we keep,
Whilst all beauty lies asleep
Hush'd be all things; no noise here
But toning of a tear:
Or a sigh of such as bring
Cowslips for her covering.

epitaph upon a virgin by
Robert Herrick 1591–1674

A vapour full of woes

Man's life's a vapour full of woes,
He cuts a caper and off he goes.

Howden, East Yorkshire

Goodbye, proud world! I'm going home:
Thou art not my friend, and I'm not thine.

Ralph Waldo Emerson, 1882

WILLIAM LEPINE
of facetious memory,
ob. the 11 March 1778,
aet. 30 years.

Alas
Where be your gibes now –
Your gambols, your flashes,
Of merriment that were wont
To set the Table in a roar?

Faversham parish church

Farewell, vain world!
I've seen enough of thee;
And careless I am what you
Can say or do to me.
I fear no Threats from
An infernal crew.
My day is past; I bid the world adieu.

Cromer, Norfolk

Here lyes the clay
Which the other day
Inclosed Sal Savill's soul,
That now is free and unconfined.
She fled and left her clog behind,
Intomb'd within this hole.

St Nicholas's, Chiswick, 1728

Here lie I, Martin Elginbrodde:
Ha'e mercy o' my soul, Lord God,
As I wad do, were I Lord God
And ye were Martin Elginbrodde.

Aberdeen

If there is a world above, he is in bliss;
If there is not he made the most of this.

Loved,
Worked,
Prayed,
Played,
With the warm urgency of young blood,
Then thanking God for all His gifts,
Passed on.

composed by an Andover man for himself

Here lies Joan Kitchener, when life was spent
She kick'd up her heels and away she went.

from ruins at Bury St Edmunds

I came in the morning – it was Spring,
And I smiled;
I walked out at noon – it was Summer,
And I was glad;
I sat me down at even – it was Autumn,
And I was sad;
I laid me down at night – it was Winter,
And I slept.

Massachusetts

Great was my grief, I could not rest;
God called me hence, He thought it best;
Unhappy marriage was my fate,
I did repent when 'twas too late.

from St Albans Abbey,
dated 1766

A married man comes nearest to the dead,
And to be buried's but to go to bed.

Samuel Butler 1612–80

Pain was my portion,
Physic was my food,
Prayer my devotion,
Drugs did me no good;
Christ came my Physician,
He knew what was best
To ease me of my pain
And take my soul to rest.

Fownhope churchyard,
Herefordshire

Of no distemper,
Of no blast he died,
But fell,
Like autumn fruit
That's mellowed long –
E'en wondered at
Because he dropped no sooner.
Providence seemed to wind him up
For four score years! yet ran he on
Nine winters more! till like a clock
Worn out with beating time,
The wheels of weary life
At last stood still.

from High Wycombe, on a man aged ninety years

EPOP NHOJ
died March 3rd, 1837,
having lived 31,755 days.
With patience to the last he did submit
And murmured not at what
the Lord thought fit;
He with Christian courage did resign
His soul to God at the appointed time.

in Stoke Damerel churchyard, Devon,
on the headstone of an under-sexton

By earth concealed, by wood confined,
And to my native dust consigned,
My grave once closed, no more I'm seen,
And nought is said but, 'She has been.'

Yoxford, Suffolk

A house she hath, it's made of such good fashion
The tenant ne'er shall pay for reparation,
Nor will her landlord ever raise the rent,
Or turn her out of doors for non-payment.
From chimney-money, too, this call is free,
To such a house who would not tenant be?

St Mary and St Eanswyth's, Folkestone

Here old John Randall lies,
Who, counting from his tale,
Liv'd three score years and ten –
Such virtue was in ale.
Ale was his meat,
Ale was his drink,
Ale did his heart revive –
And if he could have drunk his ale,
He still had been alive.

from Great Wolford, Gloucestershire,
dated 1699

EDWARD CROSTON
Have no fear,
His only fault
Was drinking beer.

Wigan, 1925

He liv'd to one hundred and five,
Sanguine and strong,
And a hundred to five
You do not live so long.

Brightwell Baldwin, near Watlington, Oxfordshire

Here under this stone
Lie Ruth and old John –
He smoked all his life
And so did his wife.
And now there's no doubt
But their pipes are both out.
Be it said without joke
That life is but smoke;
Though you live to four score,
'Tis a whiff and no more.

in Dorset, composed by a rector
upon his clerk, and dated 1752

From earth my body first arose
But here to earth again it goes.
I never desire to have it more
To plague me as it did before.

Llangerrig, Montgomeryshire

Here lies Mrs Caseys,
Who taking her aise is,
With the points of her toes
And the tip of her nose
Turned up to the roots of the dasies.

from Ireland

I was somebody.
Who, is no business
of yours.

Stowe, Vermont

Reader, pass on, nor waste your time
On bad biography and much worse rhyme,
For what I am this combious clay inures
And what I was is no affair of yours.

Ewyas Harold churchyard, Herefordshire

Those who cared for him while living
will know whose body is buried here.
To others it does not matter.

Hartford, Connecticut

Near to this stone John Barnet lies,
There's no man frets, nor no man cries;
Where he's gone, or how he fares,
There's no man knows, nor no man cares.

Betterton, Staffs

When I am dead,
Let not the day be writ –
Some will remember it!!!
Deep let it rest
In one fond female breast,
Then is my memory blest.

St Mary's, Swansea

Here Charles Rathbone he doth lie,
And by misfortune he did die
On the 17th of July,
1751.

St Giles's,
Shrewsbury, Salop

Beneath this stone old Abra'm lies,
Nobody laughs and nobody cries;
Where he's gone or how he fares
Nobody knows and no one cares.

epitaph said to have been composed for himself by
Abraham Newland, chief cashier of the Bank of
England, who died in 1807

Joseph Lee is dead and gone,
We ne'er shall see him more.
He used to wear an old drab coat,
All buttoned down before.

Mathern churchyard, Chepstow,
on the death of a familiar figure, aged 103

We were not slayne but raysd not to life but to be byried twice by men of strife. What rest could the living have when the dead had none? Agree amongst you, heere we ten are one.
Hen. Rogers, died April 17, 1641.

mysterious inscription
from Christchurch, Hampshire

Here lie I by the churchyard door.
Here lie I because I'm poor.
The farther in, the more you pay,
But here lie I as warm as they.

Carlisle, Cumbria

Near this place lyeth the body of
KATHERINE NICHOLLS
who was buried the
26th day of May 1742,
aged 70 years.
Also
JOHN MULLIS
who died in 1744,
aged 19 years.

Here we lye without the wall,
'Twas full within – they made a brawl.
Here we have not rent to pay
And yet we lye so warm as they.

inscription cut by Daniel Gumb,
Linkinhorne, Cornwall

My life's been short,
My soul has fled,
And I am numbered
With the dead.

Chigwell, Essex

Adam thus blest
(Ere by his Eve was crost)
Had surely kept
The Paradise he lost.

St Paulin, Crayford, Kent

Five times five years I lived a virgin's life;
Nine times five years I lived a virtuous wife;
Wearied of this mortal life, I rest.

1888

18 years a maiden,
1 year a wife,
1 day a mother –
Then I lost my life.

Annapolis, Nova Scotia

We do not know the pain she bore,
We did not see her die,
We only know she went away
And never said, 'Goodbye.'

Upton Pyne, near Exeter

We often sit and think of you,
We often speak your name;
There is nothing left to answer,
But your photo in the frame.

Farnham, Surrey

It is so soon that I am done for,
I wonder what I was begun for.

Cheltenham, seventeenth century

Vast strong was I, and yet did die,
And in my grave asleep I lie.
My grave is steaned round about,
But I hope the Lord will find me out.

Great Cornard, near Sudbury, Suffolk

('steaned' is from the Saxon *stean*, a stone)

What I was once fame may relate,
What I am now is each one's fate,
What I shall be none can explain,
Till He who called me calls again.

on the grave of Margaret Teasdale,
known as Meg o' Mamp Ha',
the inn immortalised
in Scott's Guy Mannering

Life is a jest,
And all things show it;
I thought so once,
And now I know it.

John Gay's epitaph for himself, 1732

Bury me not when I am dead,
Lay me not down in a dusty bed.
I could not bear the life down there
With earthworms creeping through my hair.

1883

So idle strangers pause to guess,
Passing by
With words of wondering tenderness
Or a sigh.
While she beneath her humble stone,
Waits the last call, 'unclaimed, unknown'.

Exmoor

A dreadful reckoning

Death reached the bowl and his prescription gave,
Doze now thy senses sober in the grave.
Life paid the present shot; but oh! the fears,
When morn awakes him to his long arrears,
Charged with the revels of each former day,
For there's a dreadful reckoning still to pay.

on a Cardinal, buried near Naples,
who on his last journey drank too well

Here lies the body of Betty Sexton,
Who pleased many a man but never vext one –
Unlike the woman who lies under the next stone.

Tewkesbury, Gloucestershire

Here beneath this stone there lies,
Waiting a summons to the skies,
The body of Samuel Jinking.
He was an honest Christian man,
His fault was that he took and ran
Suddenly to drinking.
Whoever reads this tablet o'er,
Take warning now and drink no more.

Maine, USA

She sleeps alone at last.

Finchingfield, Essex

Here lies 'old thirty-five percent',
The more he made, the more he lent;
The more he got, the more he craved;
The more he made, the more he shaved;
Great God! can such a soul be saved?

on a grave of a money lender,
San Francisco

Here lyes the body and the banes
Of the Laird of Whinkerstanes;
He was neither gude to rich nor puir,
And now the de'al has him sure.

in a Berwickshire churchyard

At rest beneath the churchyard stone
Lies stingy Jeremy Wyatt.
He died one morning just at ten
And saved a dinner by it.

Studley, Wiltshire

Those that knew him best
deplored him most.

1836

He was literally a father to
all the children of the parish.

Here lies my poor wife,
A sad slattern and shrew;
If I said I regretted her
I should lie too.

from a Devonshire churchyard

Here lies, thank God, a woman who
Quarrelled and stormed her whole life thro'.
Tread gently on her mouldering form,
Or else you'll raise another storm.

Staffordshire

Here lyeth the body of Martha Dias,
Always noisy, not very pious,
Who lived to the age of threescore and ten
And gave to worms what she refused to men.

from a Shropshire churchyard

Her temper was furious,
Her tongue was vindictive,
She resented a look and frowned at a smile.
She was as sour as vinegar
And punished the earth upwards of 40 years,
To say nothing of her relations.

Massachusetts

Beneath this silent Tomb is laid
A noisy, antiquated maid;
She from her cradle talked till death
And ne'er before was out of breath.

St Leonard's, Foster Lane, Cheapside, London

Here lies as silent clay
Miss Arabella Young,
Who on the 21st of May
Began to hold her tongue.

Hatfield, Massachusetts

Poorly lived – Poorly died –
Poorly buried – Nobody cried.

Lillington churchyard

Misplacing – mistaking –
Misquoting – misdating –
Men, manners, things, facts all,
Here lies Nathan Wraxall.

*George Coleman's epitaph
on the historian Sir Nathanael Wraxall, 1831*

Here lies Lord Coningsby – be civil,
The rest God knows – so does the Devil.

epitaph by Alexander Pope 1688–1744

Here lies the preacher, judge, and poet, Peter,
Who broke the laws of God, and man, and metre.

Francis, Lord Jeffrey (1773–1850)
on Peter Robinson

Battle-weary, tempest-toss'd

To the world he was a soldier,
To me he was the world.

Beneath this stone rests the body
of a British warrior,
Unknown by name or rank.

Tomb of the Unknown Soldier, 1920,
Westminster Abbey, London

Sleep on, dear Howard, in your foreign grave,
Your life for your country you nobly gave.
Though we did not see you to say goodbye,
Now in God's keeping you safely lie.

*Private Howard Pruden, Mapleton, Canada, who
died in World War 1*

When things were at their worst, he
would go up and down in the trenches
cheering the men; when danger was
greatest, his smile was loveliest.

*Edward Wyndham Tennant, 4th Battalion,
Grenadier Guards, who died in World War 1*

In loving memory of our dear brother Richard,
who went to the War in the cause of Peace and
died fighting, without hate, that love might live.

epitaph for a soldier who died in World War 1

We mourn and lament our brave youth
In one deep and national wail,
Who rushed to support our dear old flag
In its hour of deepest travail.

William P. Eames,
who died in 1863 in the American Civil War

Here sleeps in peace a Hampshire Grenadier,
Who caught his death by drinking cold small beer.
Soldiers, be wise from his untimely fall,
And when ye're hot, drink strong or none at all.
An honest soldier never is forgot,
Whether he die by musket or by pot.

erected by the officers of the garrison
in the precincts of Winchester Cathedral
to a grenadier who died in 1764

Here two young Danish Souldiers lye:
The one in quarrell chanced to die;
The other's Head, by their own Law,
With Sword was severed at one blow.

St John's Church, Beverley, Yorkshire

Sacred to the memorie of
CAPTAIN THOMAS HODGES
of the County of Somerset esquire,
who at the siege of Antwerpe aboute 1583
with unconquered courage wonne two ensignes
from the enemy when receiving his last wounde;
he gave three legacies, his soule to the Lord
Jesus, his bodye to be lodged in Flemish earth,
his heart to be sent to his dear wife in England –
Here lies his wounded heart for whome
One kingdom was too small a roome,
Two kingdoms therefore have
thought good to part
So stout a body and so brave a heart.

St Mary's, Wedmore, Somerset

Here lies one, a sailor's bride,
Who widowed was because of the tide –
It drowned her husband, so she died.

St Nicholas's, Great Yarmouth

I lost my life in the raging Seas –
A Sovereign God does as he please.
The Kittery friends they did appear
And my remains lie buried here.

Margaret Hills, 1803

Twelve times the great Atlantic cross'd,
To Fortune paying court:
In many a terrible Tempest toss'd,
But now I'm safe in Port.
Yet is my Course not ended here,
Through faith in Christ I trust,
My sins forgiv'n I shall appear
Among the Good and Just.

1784

I am grounded.

from Selby, Yorkshire,
on a sailor

Tho' Boreas' blasts and Neptune's waves
Have tossed me to and fro,
By God's decree, you plainly see,
I harbour here below,
Where I do now at anchor lie,
With many of our Fleet,
Yet once again I must set sail,
Our Admiral Christ to meet.

Swafield Church, Norfolk, dated 1808

The Old Quay Flats was my delight,
I sailed them both day and night;
God bless the Masters and the Clerks,
The packet people and flat men too,

Horse drivers and all their crew.
Our sails are set to Liverpool,
We must get underway,
Discharge our cargo safe and
Sound in Manchester Bay.
Now all hands when you go home
Neither fret, cry nor mourn,
Serve the Lord wherever you go,
Let the wind blow high or low.

This stone and grave a free gift to
JOHN YATES
Mariner Captain of the Old Quay
packet. God bless all British sailors,
Admiral Nelson and all the British
fleet. We do not know when we must
go sweet Jesus Christ to meet.

Warrington parish churchyard

This stone is sacred to the memory
of poer old
MUSTER THOMAS BOXER
who was loste in the goud boate *Rouver*
just coming home with much fishes got
near Torbay in the year of hour Lord 1722.

Prey, goud fishermen, stop and drop a tear,
For we have lost his company here,
And where he's gone we cannot tell,
But we hope far from the wicked Bell.
The Lord be with him.

Kent

Always tidy, neat and clean.
Lost his life in a submarine.

1921

Rocks and storms I'll fear no more,
When on that eternal shore.
Drop the anchor! Furl the sail!
I am safe within the Vail.

Plymouth, Devon

A woman, unclaimed, unknown,
    Washed ashore.
Just carved on the cold grey stone,
                nothing more,
Only the figures of the date –
Eighteen hundred and twenty-eight.

Over her shone the island sky,
    Soft and blue,
Close to her, fragile, sweet and shy,
    Harebells grew.
Up to her, on the sunny breeze,
Came the low laughter of the seas.

Whence did she come, who lies so still –
    Lies asleep

Under the shadow of the hill –
        While the deep
That tossed her up, a nameless waif,
Chants to her slumber, calm and safe?

Did a happy household mourn,
        Children fret,
For one who never would return,
        One missed yet?
Or does the turf of Mona cover
The darling of some yearning lover?

lines for an unidentified victim of the sea,
at Kirkmichael, Strathclyde

Long did my native powers
The dangerous ocean brave;
Protected by my God,
At home I make my grave.

1804

Graveyard humour

Here in this grave there lies a Cave;
We call a cave a grave.
If Cave be grave and grave be Cave,
Then, reader, judge, I crave,
Whether doth Cave lie here in grave,
Or grave here lie in Cave;
If grave in Cave here buried lie,
Then, grave, where is thy victory?
Go, reader, and report, here lies a Cave,
Who conquers death and buries his own grave.

Barrow-in-Furness, Leicestershire

Here lies John Bunn,
Who was killed by a gun.
His name was not Bunn,
His real name was Wood,
But that would not rhyme with gun,
So I thought Bunn would.

Warrington parish churchyard, Lancashire

Here lies at rest, I do protest,
One Chest within another;
The chest of wood was very good –
Who says so of the other?

on a clergyman named Chest

Alack and well a day
    Potter himself has turned to clay.

on Dr John Potter,
Archbishop of Canterbury, 1736

Jerusalem's curse is not fulfilled in me,
For here a stone upon a stone you see.

on Mary Stone
at Northleach in Gloucestershire, 1684

Erected to the memory of
JOHN McFARLANE
Drowned in the Water of Leith
by a few affectionate friends.

Edinburgh

Here lies Thorpe's corpse.

Bradwell-on-Sea, Essex

Here lies Sir John Plumpudding of the Grange,
Who hanged himself one morning for a change.

1794

Here lies Matthew Mudd –
Death did him no hurt;
When alive he was Mudd
And now dead he's but dirt.

Walton, Norfolk

Here lies one More, and no more than he.
One More, and no More! How can that be?
Why, one More and no more may well lie here alone,
But here lies one More and that's more than one.

St Benet's, Paul's Wharf, London

Here lies one blown and out of breath,
Who lived a merry life and died a Meredith.

on an organist name Meredith

Under this marble faire
Lies the body entomed of Gervaise Aire:
He died not of an ague fit,
Nor surfeited with too much wit.
Methinks this was a wondrous death,
That Aire should die for want of breath.

St Giles's, Cripplegate,
on one who was suffocated

Here lies John Knott.
His father was Knott before him,
He lived Knott, died Knott,
Yet underneath this stone doth lie
Knott christened, Knott begot,
And here he lies, and still is Knott.

in a Perthshire churchyard

What trifling coil we poor mortals keep;
Wake, eat, and drink, evacuate, and sleep.

Matthew Prior 1664–1721

To the memory of
EMMA AND MARY LITTLEBOY
the twin children of
George and Emma Littleboy of Hornsey.
Two Littleboys lie here,
Yet, strange to say,
These Littleboys were girls.

in a London churchyard,
dated July 16th, 1837

Oh! Sun, Moon, Stars, and ye celestial poles!
Are graves then dwindled into Buttonholes?

to one Richard Button
in a churchyard near Salisbury

Here lies Ann Mann,
She lived an old maid
And died an old Mann.

Bath Abbey

So died John So,
So so, did he so?
So did he live.
And so did he die!
So so, did he so?
And so let him lie.

Port Glasgow and written by So himself

Under the sod and under the trees
Lies the body of Jonathan Pease.
He is not here, there's only the pod:
Pease shelled out and went to God.

Nantucket, Massachusetts, 1880

Here lies John Yeast.
Pardon me for not rising.

Horsforth, West Yorkshire

Here lie Walker's particles.

on William Walker,
author of A Treatise of English Particles

Here lies Fuller's earth.

epitaph on a Dr Fuller

Beneath this sod, lies another.

Ely, Cambridgeshire

In memory of J—
Aged 787 years.

Malmesbury Abbey churchyard

Oh death, fie! fie!
To kill A. Partridge in July.

Brixham, Devon

The freshest of all Herrings once was this,
Sweet as the new-blown Rose;
In hopes of waking to eternal bliss,
Now in foul pickle she doth here repose.

Great Yarmouth, Norfolk

Does worm eat Worme? Knight Worme this
    truth confirms;
For here with worms lies Worme, a dish for worms.
Does Worme eat worm? Sure Worme will this
    deny;
For worms with Worme a dish for Worme don't
    lie.
'Tis so, and 'tis not so; for free from worms
'Tis certain Worme is blest without his worms.

Peterborough Cathedral

That he was born it cannot be denied;
He ate, drank, slept, talk'd politics, and died.

epitaph on a certain alderman
by John Cunningham 1729–73

Here lies the body of Richard Hind
Who was neither ingenious, sober, nor kind.

Spitalfields, London E1

Wha lies here?
I, Johnny Doo.
Hoo, Johnny, is that you?
Ay, man, but a'm dead noo.

Glasgow

I was buried near this dyke,
That my friends may weep as much as they like.

an epitaph by William Blake 1757–1827

Here lies an honest lawyer –
That is Strange.

Sir John Strange, Master of the Rolls,
who died in 1754

Here lies Margaret, otherwise Meg,
Who died without issue, save on her leg.
Strange woman was she, and exceedingly cunning,
For whilst one leg stood still, the other kept running.

Isle of Wight

In memeori ov
Meri Pitman,
Weif ov Mr Eizak Pitman,
Fonetik Printer ov this Siti.

epitaph composed by Sir Isaac Pitman,
inventor of shorthand, for his wife

My virtue liv's beyond the grave
My glass is rum.

should have read 'run'

Who killed Kildare? Who dared Kildare to kill?
Death kill'd Kildare, who dare kill whom he will.

epitaph for the Earl of Kildare
by Sir Thomas Wyatt 1503–42

Here X. lies dead, but God's forgiving,
And shows compassion to the living.

an epitaph by
J. E. Thorold Rogers 1823–90

Here I lie for the last time;
Lying has been my pastime,
And now I've joined the heavenly choir
I hope I still may play my lyre.

epitaph on an Irish priest

Here lies the body of W. W.,
Who never more will trouble you, trouble you.

Lincoln's Inn Fields, London WC2

Gone to be an angle.

should have read 'angel'

Down the lanes of memory
The lights are never dim;
Until the stars forget to shine
We shall remember her.

Morecambe, Lancashire

Lord, she were thin.

> *should have read 'thine'.*
> *The stonemason, asked to add the*
> *missing e, revised the inscription to read:*
> *Ee, Lord, she were thin.*

Here lies my poor wife, without bed or blanket;
Bur dead as doornail; God be thanked.

> *Olney, Buckinghamshire*

Here lies my poor wife, much lamented;
She is happy, and I am contented.

Andover, Hampshire

In short . . .

Now Ain't That Too Bad.

1907

The Chisel Can't Help Her Any.

1923

Been Here
and Gone There.
Had a Good Time.

1931

Going, But Know Not Where.

1918

Belgium me birth, Britaine me breeding gave;
Cornwall a wife, ten children, and a grave.

St Madron

He's gone, too.

*at the foot of a stone on
which a husband had recorded the virtues of
the wife he had buried in a Fulham churchyard*

THOMAS WOOD
Formerly a Bather at this Place.

St John's Church, Margate

And there was a great calm!

Sandbach, Cheshire

Anything for a change.

Eastbourne, Sussex

CHARLES LEWIS
He voted for Abraham Lincoln.

1865

He meant well,
Tried a little, failed much.

1889

She was good but not brilliant,
Useful but not great.

1807

Gone home.

Harrogate, Yorkshire

He sowed, others reaped.

1895

Persecuted for wearing a beard,

Joseph Palmer, who died in 1873

Came in,
Walked about,
Didn't like it,
Walked out.

Suffolk

I always got a bear here.

on the grave of a
Long Island huntsman,
buried in a favourite hunting ground

That life is long, which answers life's great end.

1821

The Lord don't make any mistakes.

1904

Here's the last end of the Mortal Story –
He's Dead.

Daniel Hoar, who died in 1773, aged 93

She lived – what more can then be said:
She died – and all we know she's dead.

1836

Here lies the body of Daniel Saul,
Spitalfields weaver, and that's all.

1798

Upon the man who's buried here
Drop anything except a tear.

Boot, Cumbria

This one's on me.

*on the headstone
of a popular host and wit
of Rhode Island, USA, 1938*

I told you I was sick.

1904

Where is God?

1895

Something rich and strange

Nothing of him that doth fade,
But doth suffer a sea-change
Into something rich and strange.

Percy Bysshe Shelley,
who was drowned in 1822
(a quotation from Shakespeare's The Tempest*)*

Here's one in whom Nature feared – faint at
                                    such vying –
Eclipse while he lived, and decease at his dying.

Cardinal Bembo's
epitaph on Raphael, 1520

When a whirlwind hath blown the dust of the Churchyard into the Church, and the man sweeps out the dust of the Church into the Churchyard, who will undertake to sift those dusts again, and to pronounce: This is the Patrician, this is the noble flower, and this the yeomanly, this the Plebeian bran.

John Donne

Good friend, for Jesus sake forbeare
To dig the dust enclosed heare:
Bleste be ye man [tha]t spare these stones,
And curst be he [tha]t moves my bones.

William Shakespeare (1564–1616),
Stratford-upon-Avon

Time held me green and dying
Though I sang in my chains like the sea.

Dylan Thomas (1914–53),
Poet's Corner, Westminster Abbey
(quotation from 'Fern Hill')

Here lies our Sovereign Lord the King
Whose word no man relies on,
Who never said a foolish thing
Nor ever did a wise one.

Rochester on Charles II

Reader, should you reflect on his errors,
Remember his many virtues
And that he was a mortal.

Sir Walter Raleigh,
who was beheaded in 1618

Beneath this stone a Poet Laureate lies,
Nor great, nor good, nor foolish, nor yet wise;
Not meanly humble, nor yet swell'd with pride,
He simply liv'd – and just as simply died;
Each year his Muse produc'd a Birthday Ode,
Compos'd with flattery in the usual mode:
For this, and but for this, to George's praise,
The Bard was pension'd and received the bays.

on William Whitehead (1715–85)

Here lyes the body of Edmund Spenser, the
Prince of Poets in his tyme, whose Divine
Spirit needs noe other witnesse than the
workes which he left behinde him.

Westminster Abbey

Here lies the body of Jonathan Swift,
Doctor of Divinity, Dean of this Cathedral Church.
Gone where wild rage can tear the heart no more.
Go, traveller, and imitate if you can an earnest
Manly champion of freedom.

epitaph of Jonathan Swift (1667–1745)
on his tomb in St Patrick's Cathedral, Dublin

Soyer is gone! Then be it said,
Indeed, indeed, great Pan is dead.

on the celebrated chef Alexis Soyer, 1858

Here lies Nolly Goldsmith, for shortness
call'd Noll,
Who wrote like an angel, but talk'd like
poor Poll.

epitaph on Oliver Goldsmith by David Garrick,
1774

Whilst Butler, needy wretch! was yet alive,
No generous patron would a dinner give;
See him, when starved to death and turned to dust,
Presented with a monumental bust.
The poet's fate is here in emblem shewn –
He asked for bread and he received a stone.

on the monument to
Samuel Butler (1612–80)
in Westminster Abbey

Under this stone, Reader, survey
Dead Sir John Vanbrugh's house of clay.
Lie heavy on him, Earth, for he
Laid many heavy loads on thee!

epitaph on
Sir John Vanbrugh (1664–1726)
playwright and architect

Here lies Piron – a man of no position,
Who was not even an Academician.

epitaph for himself by Alexis Piron, 1689–1773

Underneath this stone
Lies Robert Earl of Hungtindon.
No archer was as him so good,
And people called him Robin Hood,
And such archers as him and his men
Will England never see again.

on the grave Robin Hood,
the celebrated outlaw, who died in 1247
and was buried in Kirklees Abbey, Yorkshire

Here lies one whose name was writ in water.

John Keats, 1821

Nature and Nature's laws lay hid in night –
God said, Let Newton be, and all was light.

Pope on Sir Isaac Newton

Posterity will ne'er survey
A nobler grave than this:
Here lie the bones of Castlereagh –
Stop, traveller, and piss.

Byron on Castlereagh

The body of
BENJAMIN FRANKLIN,
printer
Like the cover of an old book,
Its contents worn out
And stripped of its lettering and gilding,
Lies here, food for worms!
Yet the work itself shall not be lost,
For it will, as he believed, appear once more
In a new
And more beautiful edition,
Corrected and amended
By its Author!

Boston, USA, 1728

Born in America, in Europe bred,
In Africa travelled and in Asia wed –
Where long he lived and thrived. In London dead.
Much good, some ill, he did so hope all's even,
And that his soul through mercy's gone to heaven.
You that survive and read this tale take care
For this most certain exit to prepare,
Where blest in peace the actions of the just
Smell sweet and blossom in the silent dust.

*Wrexham, on the tomb of Eliugh Yale,
founder of Yale University, USA*

Their grief is in proportion to their affection, they know their loss to be irreparable, but in their deepest affliction they are consoled by a firm though humble hope that her charity, devotion, faith and purity rendered her soul acceptable in the sight of her Redeemer.

epitaph for Jane Austin (1775–1817)

I know what *should* be put on my tomb:
Died of the Neglect of his
Correspondence and Consequent Consciencitis.

Robert Louis Stevenson in a letter dated 1885

Under the wide and starry sky
Dig the grave and let me lie.
Glad did I live and gladly die,
   And I laid me down with a will.

This be the verse you grave for me:
Here he lies where he longed to be;
Home is the sailor, home from sea
   And the hunter home from the hill.

Robert Louis Stevenson (1850–94)

If I should die, think only this of me:
　　That there's some corner of a foreign field
That is for ever England. There shall be
　　In that rich earth a richer dust concealed;
A dust whom England bore, shaped, made aware,
　　Gave, once, her flowers to love, her ways to roam,
A body of England's, breathing English air,
　　Washed by the rivers, blest by suns of home.

And think, this heart, all evil shed away,
　　A pulse in the eternal mind, no less
　　　　Gives somewhere back the thoughts by
　　　　　　　　　　　　England given;
Her sights and sounds; dreams happy as her day;
　　And laughter, learnt of friends; and gentleness
　　　In hearts at peace, under an English heaven.

Rupert Brooke (1887–1915)

Patriotism is not enough; I must have
no hatred or bitterness for anyone.

last words of Edith Cavell,
British Red Cross nurse who died in 1915

When I am dead I hope it may be said –
His sins were scarlet but his books were read.

suggested by Mr Hilaire Belloc for himself

If I take the Wings of the Morning,
and Dwell in the Uttermost Parts of the Sea . . .

Charles Lindbergh (1902–74),
quoting from Psalm 139, verse 9

May the Divine Spirit that Animated
Babe Ruth to Win the Crucial Game of Life
Inspire the Youth of America!

George Herman ('Babe') Ruth (1895–1948)

First to go through the
Whirlpool Rapids in a barrel and live.

Carlisle D. Graham,
who died in Niagara Falls, New York, 1886

Here lies Groucho Marx –
and Lies and Lies and Lies.
PS. He never kissed an ugly girl.

Groucho Marx (1895–1977)

Heap dustbins on him:
They'll not meet
The apex of his self-conceit.

Thomas Hardy on George Moore

Excuse my dust.

Dorothy Parker (1893–1967)

My son was killed while laughing at some jest.
I would I knew
What it was, and it might serve me in a time
when jests are few.

Rudyard Kipling on his son,
killed in the First World War

Safe lodged within his blanket, here below,
Lie the last relics of old Orono;
Worn down with toil and care, he in a trice
Exchanged his wigwam for a paradise.

Penobscot chief, who died in 1801

For beauty, wit, for sterling sense,
For temper mild, for eloquence,
For courage bold, for things wartegan,
He was the glory of Moheagan –
Whose death has caused great lamentation
Both to ye English and ye Indian Nation.

Samuel Uncas, Mohican chief

God wills us free – man wills us slaves.
I will as God wills, God's will be done.
Here lies the body of John Jack,
A native of Africa, who died March 1773,
Aged about sixty years.
Though born in a land of slavery
He was born free,
Though he lived in a land of liberty
He lived a slave
Till, by his honest though stolen labours,
He acquired the source of slavery,
Which gave him his freedom –
Though not before
Death the great tyrant

Gave him his final emancipation
And put him on a footing with kings.
Though a slave to vice
He practised those virtues
Without which kings are but slaves.

Concord, Massachusetts

FREE AT LAST, FREE AT LAST!
THANK GOD ALMIGHTY,
I'M FREE AT LAST.

Reverend Dr Martin Luther King Jr,
South View Cemetery, Atlanta, Georgia, 1968

To the memory of the man, first in
war, first in peace, and first in the
hearts of his countrymen.

George Washington,
Mount Vernon, Virginia, 1779

When terrestrial, all in chaos shall exhibit
    effervescense,
Then celestial virtues, in their most refulgent
    brilliant essence,
Shall with beaming beautious radiance thro' the
    ebullition shine;
Transcending to glorious regions beatifical
    sublime;
Human power absorbed deficient to delineate
    such effulgent lasting spirits;
Where honest plebians ever will have precedence
    over
Ambiguous great monarchs.

High Ercall, Shropshire

Cast a cold Eye
On Life, on Death.
Horseman pass by!

W. B. Yeats (1865–1939)

In sure and certain hope

To die, is but to live for ever.

1835

The less of this cold world, the more of Heaven:
The briefer life, the earlier Immortality.

Toronto, Canada

Why do we mourn departing friends
Or shake at death's alarms?
'Tis but the voice that Jesus sends
To call them to his arms.

1814

Adieu, my friends, weep not for me!
Long have I stemmed life's troubled sea,
But now redeem'd from sin and woe
I rest where peaceful waters flow.

1844

Here lyeth Sara Young
who went to sleep
with Christ
on the 6th of January, 1741.

Liverpool

Having the day before her death most
devoutly received ye Holy Communion
(wch she said she would not have omitted
for ten thousand worlds), she was vouchsafed
in a miraculous manner an immediate prospect
of her future blisse for ye space of two houres
to ye astonishment of all about her, and being
(like St Paul) in an inexpressible transport of
joy (thereby fully evidencing her foresight of
the heavenly glory) in inconceivable raptures
triumphing over death and continuing
sensible to ye last, she resigned her pious
soul to God and victoriously entered into rest,
Oct. 11, anno dom. 1687, aetatis suae 21.

All Saints, Hollingbourne, Kent

Grieve not, dear friends, but be content
For unto you we were but lent;
Our years on earth they were but few –
We wasted like the morning dew.
When death was sent from God above,
So suddenly to part our Love,
No friends nor yet Physician's Art
Could then prevent his fatal Dart.
Comfort yourselves and be content,
A soul with Christ do not lament.

1802

Here I Lie

1790

Weep not, my friends, as you pass by,
Beneath this stone my body lies,
My soul is gone in yonder skies,
To live with those that's glad to die.

1874

Here lies a Superior Person, in
intelligent anticipation of the life to come.

Lord Curzon,
composed for himself in whimsical mood

Reader, take notice
that on ye 12 February 1760
THOS. CORBISHLEY,
a brave veteran dragoon,
here went into his winter quarters.
But remember that when the trumpet calls,
He'll out and march again.

I rest in hope til Christ shall come,
I feare not death, nor day of dome;
Though earth cover me
Death cannot devour me;
Christ mine and thine,
Our meeting a happie greeting;
O merrie last day, wellcome, wellcome,
Lord, I will bowe and thou shalt beate,
Deliver me from hell heate.
O Death, where is thy sting?
O grave, where is thy victorie?
Thankes to my Lord Christ
They cannot hurt me.

composed for herself by Jane Docwra,
who died in 1645 at Pirton in Hertfordshire

God gave me at Kennardington in Kent
My native breath which now alas is spent;
My parents gave me Tilden Smith for name,
I to the Park Farm in this parish came,
And there for many lingering years did dwell
Whilst my good neighbours did respect me well.
But now, my friends, I go by nature's call,
In humble hope my crimes will measure small;
Years following years steal something every day
And lastly steal us from ourselves away;
Life's span forbids us to extend our cares
And stretch our hopes beyond our fleeting years.
Mary Fermenger, my Wife, from Peasmarsh Place,
Lies mouldering here, likewise in hope of grace.

from Bodiam, Sussex, dated 1789

Rest in peace
until we meet again.

1864

Here landed, the proceeds of that we ventured,
In Nature's Custom House this dust is entered;
Christ's all our gaine by whom in death we live
And carry hence that only which we give;
Almes deeds are secret bills at sight (the rest
On Heaven's exchange is subject to protest);
This uncorruptible manna of the Just
Is lasting store, exempt from worms and dust.

St Peter and St Paul's, Lynsted, Kent

Let no proud stone with sculptured virtues rise
To mark the spot wherein a sinner lies,
But if some boast must deck the sinner's grave,
Boast of His Love, Who died lost man to save.
And when life's journey is over,
And I the dear Saviour shall see,
I'll praise him for ever and ever,
For saving a sinner like me.

on the grave of a master printer in Norwich

Death is not an eternal sleep,
Therefore my friends you need not weep;
But look by faith beyond the grave,
That you some peace of soul may have.

1803

Body – I Mary Pawson lye below sleeping;
Soul – I Mary Pawson sitte above waking;
Both – We hope to meet again with glory clothed –
Then will Mary Pawson be for evermore blessed.
She lived 70 years and dyed 1599.

St Giles' Cripplegate, London

Surviving friends, although you mourn,
Let this console, I shall return:
The righteous judge can by his word
Bring me triumphing with the Lord.

Buxton, Derbyshire

Contente thyselfe with patience.
With Christ to beare the Crosse of paine,
Which can and will bring recompense
A thousandfoold with like gaine,
Let nothing cause the harte to qualle;
Launche out the boote,
Hayle upp the saille,
Put from the earthy shoore,
And at the length thou shalt obtaine
Unto the part that shall remaine
For ever more.

Beaconsfield parish church, dated 1572

We part to meet again –
What a joyful thought.

Chicago, Illinois

Here lieth one of Abel's race
Whom Cain did hunt from place to place;
Yet not dismayed about he went
Working until his days were spent.
He is now at rest and takes a nap
Upon their Common Mother's lap,
Waiting to hear ye bridegroom say,
Arise, my love, and come away.

Goirlon Chapel, near
Abergavenny, Monmouthshire

With Christ, which is far better.
Brompton Cemetery, London, 1880

I am innocent and God will
clear my innocency.

Rebecca Nurse,
accused of witchcraft and
hanged in Salem, Massachusetts, in 1692

Why should we tremble to convey
Their bodies to the tomb
Where Jesus our dear saviour lay
And left a long perfume?

Cape Cod, Massachusetts, 1813

The Spiritual Railway

The line to Heaven by Christ was made:
With heavenly truth the rails are laid;
From Earth to Heaven the line extends,
To life eternal where it ends.
Repentance is the station then
Where passengers are taken in;
No fee for them is there to pay
For Jesus is himself the way.
God's word is the first engineer,
It points the way to heaven so dear.
Through tunnels dark and dreary here
It does the way to glory steer.
God's love the fire, his truth the steam

Which drives the engine and the train.
All you who would to glory ride,
Must come to Christ, in him abide.
In first and second and third class,
Repentance, faith and holiness,
You must the way to glory gain
Or you with Christ will not remain.
Come then, poor sinners, now's the time,
At any station on the line,
If you'll repent and turn from sin,
The train will stop and take you in.

from Ely Cathederal,
in memory of William Pickering
who died December 24th 1845 aged
30 years and Richard Edger who died
December 24th 1845 aged 24 years.

Stones weep though eyes be dry,
Choicest flowers soonest die;
Their sun oft sets at noon
Whose fruit is ripe in June.
Then tears of joy be thine,
Since earth must soon resign
To God what is divine.

Balquhidder churchyard, Perthshire

Here lies the body of Sarah,
wife of John Hays,who died
24th March 1823 AD, aged 42 years.
The Lord giveth and the Lord taketh away.
Blessed is the name of the Lord

Cupar, Fife

One night awaits us all

One night awaits us all:
Death's road we all must go.

quoted from Horace, 1752

O reader, be prepared.

1891

This world's a city with many a crooked street,
And Death the Market Place where all men meet.
If Life were merchandise that men could buy,
The rich would live and none but poor would die.

at Nutfield, Surrey, on a grave dated 1660

Let your wind go free,
Wherever you be,
For the keeping it in
Was the death of me.

Brixham, Devon

Our life is but a winter's day:
Some only breakfast and away;
Others to dinner stay and are full fed;
The oldest man but sups and goes to bed.
Large is his debt who lingers out the day,
Who goes the soonest has the least to pay.

Linslade, Buckinghamshire

Farewell, vain earth, I've had enough of thee,
And now I'm careless what they say'st of me;
Thy smiles I car'st not, nor thy frowns I fear –
My care is past, my head lies quiet here.
What faults you see in me take care to shun,
And look at home – enough is to be done.

epitaph chosen by a London publican

How loved, how valued once avails thee not,
To whom related or by whom begot;
A heap of dust alone remains of thee –
'Tis all thou are, and what we all must be.

1706

Although she is dead she invites you to view
Her stone in the churchyard and read it with care;
Remember it is nothing before our bodies lie
As there she lies moulding and turning to clay.

Tarrytown, New York, 1814

Stay, Passenger, awhile and read your doome –
I am as you must be, dead.

Branscombe, Devon

These lines are not to praise the dead,
But to admonish those by whom they're read.
Whatever his failings were, leave them alone,
And use thine utmost care to mend thine own.

from Worstead churchyard, Norfolk

My Name, my Country, what are they to thee?
What whether high or low my pedigree?
Perhaps I far surpassed all other men,
Perhaps I fell below them all, what then?
Suffice it, stranger, that thou seest a tomb,
Thou know'st its use, it hides – no matter whom.

Cheran, South Carolina

Strong and at labour
Suddenly he reels,
Death came behind him
And stroke up his heels.

Such sudden stroke,
surviving mortals bid ye,
Stand on your watch,
And do be also ready.

from Branscombe,
Devon, on a farmer who
is said to have died suddenly while
sheepshearing in 1673

The morning sun on me arose –
At night I took my last repose.
Let my quick fate a warning be
To all who pass my grave to see.

Evesham, Worcestershire

Here lie I by the chancel door,
Here lie I because I'm poor,
The farther in, the more you'll pay,
Here lie I as warm as they.

Kingsbridge, South Devon

Behold and See,
For as I am So shalt Thou Be,
And as Thou Art
So Once Was I.
Be Sure of This –
That Thou Must Die.

1709

Here lies interred a blooming youth,
Who lived in love and died in truth.
Behold and see as you pass by,
As you are now so once was I,
As I am now so you must be;
Prepare for death and follow me.

1794

My time is come – next may be thine,
Prepare for it whilst thou hast time;
And that thou mayst preparèd be,
Live unto Him who died for thee.

1874

A sov'reign God, who set my bounds,
Did quickly take my breath.
Be ready then each hour you live
To meet an instant death.

1791

Remember this as you walk round,
All must return into the ground;
For by transgression in the garden
Adam did receive his warning;
And as God's word does prove true,
I have returned, and so must you.

Ridgefield, Connecticut

Remember me, as you pass by,
As you are now, so once was I,
And as I am so you must be,
So prepare thyself to follow me.
[*To which was added by a wag*]
To follow you I'm not content
Until I know which way you went.

Grantham, Lincolnshire

Go, Reader,
And in the short Space of Life allotted thee
Attend to his Examples
And Imitate his Virtues.

New Haven, Connecticut, 1775

Seize, mortals, seize the transient hour,
Improve each moment as it flies;
Life's a short Summer, man a flower;
He dies – Alas! how soon he dies.

1816

Seize the moments while they stay;
Seize them, use them,
Lest you lose them
And lament the wasted day.

Ludlow, Shropshire

Keep death and judgment always in your eye,
Or else the devil off with you will fly,
And in his kiln with brimstone ever fry:
If you neglect the narrow road to seek,
Christ will reject you, like a half-burnt brick!

1827

Be thou what you think I ought to have been.

1842

Reader, pass on and ne'er waste your time
On bad biography and bitter rhyme,
For what I am this cumb'rous clay insures,
And what I was, is no affair of yours.

1797

Weep not for me, for it is in vain,
Weep for your sins, and then refrain.

1708

There was hope in his end.
May there be hope in thine.

1803

Man comes into the world naked and bare,
He travels through life with trouble and care,
His exit from the world takes him no one
                                       knows where;
If it's well with him here, it is well with him there.

1817

When Spring was seen my life was green
For I was blithe and young;
When Summer smiled my hopes beguiled
My heart was hale and strong;
When Autumn crowned with fruits came round
I entertained no fear;
There rose at last a Wintry blast
And then they laid me here.

Santon, near Douglas, Isle of Man

Prepare for this change. Thou canst not tell when thy looking eye will shut for ever. From here 'tis plain youth hath no surety. Think on this event. What thou dost lay up for it will be a precious treasure to thee, when the soul with all its keenest faculties must travel. Whither? Has thou not thought? If not let not a moment pass thee. At that time thou wilt know a moment's value.

Elizabeth Bucklee, 1790,
St Giles' Cripplegate, London

In sixteen hundred and ninety-three
GEORGE WOOD OF CHEADLE
set this tree.
Then he was alive but now he's dead:
Up to this stone he lays his head.
Be shure you have account to give
When you are dead how you did live.

Cheadle, Staffordshire

I dreamt that buried in my bed of clay
Close by a common beggar's side I lay;
Such a mean companion hurt my pride
And like a corpse of consequence I cried:
Scoundrel, begone, and henceforth touch me not,
More manners learn, and at a distance rot.
Scoundrel, in still haughtier tones cried he,
Proud lump of earth, I scorn thy words and thee:
All here are equal, thy place now is mine;
This is my rotting place, and that is thine.

Providence, Rhode Island, 1835

Stop, courteous passenger, till thou hast read –
The living may gain knowledge by the dead.
Five times five years I lived a virgin's life.
Ten times five years I lived a virtuous wife,
Ten times five years I wept a widow's woes,
Now, tired of mortal life, I here repose.
Eight mighty kings of Scotland and one queen
I 'twixt my cradle and my grave have seen,
Four times five years the Commonwealth I saw;
Ten times the subjects rise against the law;
Twice have I seen old Prelacy pulled down,
And twice the cloak was humbled by the gown;
I saw my country sold for English ore,
And Stuart race destroyed to rise no more.
Such desolations in my time have been,
I have an end of all perfection seen.

on the tomb of Margaret Scott,
who died at Dalkeith in 1738

God plants his flowers when he
thinks fit; then plucks at any age.

Pitcairn, Grandtully, Perthshire

A stranger walking in the garden observed a
flower cut down, and complained that a plant
so useful, with blossoms so beautiful, should be
destroyed. The gardener replied, 'The Master
came, he cut it down.' No more was said.

Norwich Cemetery

Who would live in others' breath?
Fame deceives the dead man's trust.
Since our names are chang'd in death,
Sand I was, and now am dust.

epitaph for Johannis Sande

Here lies the great. False marble, where?
Nothing but sordid dust lies there.

Bath

I'm Smith of Stoke, aged sixty-odd;
   I've lived without a dame
From youth-time on: and would to God
   My dad had done the same.

epitaph on a pessimist by
Thomas Hardy 1840–1928

This is the grave of Mike O'Day
Who died maintaining his right of way.
His right was clear, his will was strong,
But he's just as dead as if he'd been wrong.

epitaph by W. B. Yeats 1865–1939

A world I did not wish to enter
Took me and poised me on my centre,
Made me grimace, and foot, and prance,
As cats on hot bricks have to dance
Strange jigs to keep them from the floor,
Till they sink down and feel no more.

a necessitarian's epitaph by
Thomas Hardy 1840–1928

Words from dying lips

I should never have switched from Scotch to
　　Martinis.

　　　　　　　Humphrey Bogart, *film actor*

Either this wallpaper goes or I do.

　　　　　　　Oscar Wilde, *dramatist*

Oh, I'm so bored with it all.

　　　　　　　Winston Churchill, *British prime minister*

Doctor, do you think it could have been the
sausage?

Paul Claudel, *French writer*

I've had eighteen straight whiskies, I think that's
a record . . . after thirty-nine years, this is all
I've done.

Dylan Thomas, *poet*

Goodnight, my darlings, I'll see you tomorrow.
Noël Coward, *British playwright*

I wish to be buried standing – facing Germany.
Georges Clemenceau, *French premier*

Am I dying, or is this my birthday?
Nancy Astor, *British politician*

That was the best ice-cream soda I ever tasted.
Lou Costello, *American comedian*

I suppose I am now becoming a god.
Vespasian, *Roman emperor*

That was a great game of golf, fellers.
Bing Crosby, *American singer*

I am sweeping through the gates, washed in the
blood of the lamb.
Alexander II, *Russian tsar*

The bullet hasn't been made that can kill me.
Legs Diamond, *gangster*

On the whole, I'd rather be in Philadelphia.
W. C. Fields, *American comedian*

Carry my bones before you on your march, for the rebels will not be able to endure the sight of me.

Edward I, *King of England*

Now I'll have *eine kleine* pause.
Kathleen Ferrier, *opera singer*

Get my swan costume ready.

Anna Pavlova, *ballerina*

Let's do it.

Gary Gilmore,
American murderer about to be executed

I hope to see you on Tuesday at 10.30 a.m.

Earl Haig, *British general*

I regret that I have but one life to give for my
country.

Nathan Hale, *American soldier*

Four sixes to beat.

John Wesley Hardin, *American outlaw*

I am about the extent of a tenth of a gnat's
eyebrow better.

Joel Chandler Harris, *American author*

Cheer up, children, I'm all right.
Franz Joseph Haydn, *composer*

That picture is crooked.
Jesse James, *bank and train robber*

Go away. I'm all right.

H. G. Wells, *author*

I think it is time for morphine.

D. H. Lawrence, *British author*

Strike the tent.

Robert E. Lee, *Confederate general*

I can't live any longer with my nerves.

Jean Seberg,
US film star who committed suicide

Keep Paddy behind the big mixer.
                    Alfred McAlpine, *British building tycoon*

Now I have finished with all earthly business, and
   high time too.
                        Franz Lehár, *Hungarian composer*

They couldn't hit an elephant at this dist . . .
                    John Sedgwick, *US general*

I love the rain, I want the feeling of it on my face.
Katherine Mansfield, *writer*

Last words are for fools who haven't said enough.
Karl Marx, *philosopher*

So little done, so much to do.
Cecil Rhodes, *South African statesman*

Dying is a very dull, dreary affair. My advice to
you is to have nothing whatever to do with it.
William Somerset Maugham, *British writer*

I am crossing a beautiful wide river and the
opposite shore is coming nearer and nearer.
George Meade, *US Civil War general*

Ah, my God, I am dead.
Catherine de Medici, *Florentine ruler*

Put that bloody cigarette out.
H. H. Munro ('Saki'), *British author*

I shall soon know the grand secret.
Arthur Thistlewood,
English conspirator about to be hanged

But, but, Mr Colonel . . .
Benito Mussolini, *Italian dictator*

Oh God, here I go . . .
Max Baer, heavyweight boxer

Die, my dear doctor, that's the last thing I shall do.
Viscount Palmerston, British prime minister

What is the scaffold? A short cut to heaven.
Charles Peace, murderer

If this is dying, I don't think much of it.

Lytton Strachey, *biographer*

I think I could eat one of Bellamy's veal pies.

William Pitt (the younger),
British prime minister

Turn up the lights, I don't want to go home in the dark.

William Porter (O. Henry),
US short-story writer

I could wish this tragic scene were over, but I
hope to go through it with becoming dignity.
James Quin, *Irish actor*

Let down the curtain, the farce is over.
François Rabelais, *French writer*

I have a terrific headache.
Franklin D. Roosevelt, *US president*

You can keep the things of bronze and stone and give me one man to remember me just once a year.

Damon Runyon, *American writer*

Gentlemen of the jury, you may retire.

Charles Tenterden, *Lord Chief Justice*

I am dying as I have lived: beyond my means.

Oscar Wilde, *dramatist*